BIG GIRLS DON'T CRY

BIG GIRLS DON'T CRY

A Memoir About Taking Up Space

Susan Swan

Foreword by Margaret Atwood

Beacon Press, Boston

BEACON PRESS
Boston, Massachusetts
www.beacon.org

Beacon Press books
are published under the auspices of
the Unitarian Universalist Association of Congregations.

28 27 26 25   8 7 6 5 4 3 2 1

This book is printed on acid-free paper that meets the uncoated paper
ANSI/NISO specifications for permanence as revised in 1992.

Big Girls Don't Cry is a memoir based on the author's life experiences as
she recollects them. Some names and details have been changed.

Photo on half-title page courtesy of the Huronia Museum,
accession number (2006.0020.4571).

Library of Congress Cataloging-in-Publication Data is available for this title.
ISBN: 978-0-8070-2258-0; e-book: 978-0-8070-2259-7
audiobook: 978-0-8070-2283-2

For my pod—Sam, Pieter, Jane, Thom,
and my husband, Patrick

I was the tall girl, that whole thing . . . I just desperately wanted to be like the girls I saw, the peppy cheerleaders . . . so many of us are living in a world where we feel othered. . . . That's why it's so important for us to put our stories out there.

—MICHELLE OBAMA

FOREWORD

SUSAN SWAN'S MEMOIR, *Big Girls Don't Cry*, is a book
I myself never could have written. Why? Because I'm short. I
wasn't short in 1955, when I was fifteen—five-four was the
average height for girls then. Those over five-eight were thought
of as gangly and spindly, giants who found it hard to get dates—
boys were shorter at that time too. Such unlucky girls were told
to stand up straight and not hunch, because they were always
hugging their schoolbooks to their chests and walking in a semi-
crouch, trying to seem littler than they were.

Why would they have wanted that? I think now. *To be short!*
When Susan Swan told me she had once been attacked by a man
intent on nefarious acts but had picked him up and thrown him
against the wall, I thought, *Wow!* Only in my dreams could I ever
have done that! Kicking in the nuts, yes; that would have been
possible for me. But not wall-throwing. I have a fairly tall and muscular cousin who'd once been chased into a field in Italy, along
with her friend, by two lust-lorn guys. "What did you do?" I said.
"We hit them on the heads with our suitcases," she said, laughing, "and they ran away." I wouldn't have been able to get up high
enough for a head shot with a suitcase.

So of course I wanted to read about what it must have been
like to be so tall. Imposing! Statuesque! Able to wear wide cinch

belts gracefully and sport fashion-model clothes—maybe even shoulder pads!—without looking like SpongeBob SquarePants. Also, with such a height I myself could have been more insouciant. Not prone to looking over my shoulder, or not as much. Able to saunter less cautiously through life than us shorties. Not having to climb a step stool to get the dishes down off the top shelf. There would have been disadvantages, such as trying to cram oneself into an airplane seat and bumping one's head on the tops of fifteenth-century doorways, but on the whole . . .

"You should write about that part of your life," I told Susan. "About being so tall."

"Who'd want to read about that?" she said. I'd known Susan since—when?—the late seventies, when she'd been a hotshot arts reporter and had interviewed me over some book or other that I'd been publishing. She remembers me in a black cape, looking like something out of a Victorian melodrama; I remember her as a blond bombshell, reminiscent of a prima donna in a Wagnerian opera. We'd struck up an unlikely friendship and kept it up over the ensuing thirty-five or forty years, so naturally she was sharing the idea for her latest project with me.

By 2018, she'd embarked on an earnest book called *Letters to a Young Feminist*, a more serious and worthy venture than a reminiscence about her body size, in her view. She was going to explain to the young feminists what the feminist thing had been like back in the seventies when she'd been a youngish feminist herself, and do some tut-tutting about the reckless and harmful way some of the younger gen had been going about their emotion-driven and fact-averse believe-all-women activism. (It is not now and never was true that there aren't any female con artists, fakers, opportunists, liars, narcissists, and psychopaths. There are fewer female serial killers and murderous dictators, however, which is some consolation, I suppose.)

In this work-in-progress—of which I was a first-draft reader— Susan had included a little but not nearly enough material about her own earlier life, a life that had been unusual, to put it mildly. Not everyone had engaged in performance art pieces by posing as the goddess Diana while standing semi-nude in a public fountain. (Tall girls were naturals for such roles: one of the signs of divinity, according to the ancient Greeks, was unusual height.) Then there was the duel with fencing foils . . .

"Forget the young feminists," I said. "Nobody likes unsolicited advice, so they won't thank you for it. Anyway, by the time you get the book finished, your intended audience won't be young anymore, and their views may well have changed, and there will be a whole new generation of young feminists who will find some of the present crop ridiculous. That's how it goes. Instead, why don't you write a memoir about being tall? Gift and curse! The pluses as well as the minuses! I'd read that, but the advice to young feminists not so much." At first Susan thought the height book was a "goofy" idea, but eventually she saw the beauty of it and set to work. "The more I thought about it," she told me, "the more I realized my size has affected everything in my life: my feelings about being a woman, my relationships, and my writing. In some ways, this memoir is a pilgrim's progress of a woman with a large body making her way in the world." "Sounds good to me," I said. "What are you going to call it?" Many titles were discussed, including *Bigger*—but this title then appeared as a movie, and anyway it implied she was bulky—and *Higher* (my suggestion), which made her sound like a weed addict, as her partner quipped, accurately. Susan came up with *Too Tall*, and then *Too Big*, which seemed a bit negative to me—too tall or too big for what, and for whom? Too tall and big for the ideas of most people about how much space a female person ought to take up, I suppose. There had been occasions on which Susan had been mistaken for a man in drag.

I continued to muse. Too tall, or larger than life? Too big, or just right? *Pilgrim's Progress*, trudging through the Slough of Despond and battling the Giant Despair, or *Some Like It Hot and Also Tall*, a sex-and-romance romp with love-smitten playboys and freely flowing champagne? ("Never married men, though," Susan said virtuously.) So could "too big" possibly be a lot of fun once a girl gets used to it and defeats the critical voices in her head? I somehow can't help seeing Susan—in some of her phases—as the central figure in the Rockettes kick line: gorgeous, glamourous, and the focal point holding it all together. If people are going to stare at you anyway, you might as well put on a good show.

After I'd invested much thought and many literary illusions in *Too Big*, Susan changed her mind again. *Big Girls Don't Cry* would be her title! Seems that she thought it was a better way to show how people have always matched her size with the expectation that she'd handle whatever came her way.

Either title brings to mind—or to my mind—the scene in *Alice's Adventures in Wonderland* in which Alice eats too much of the magic mushroom, grows gigantic, and finds herself crammed into a tiny room with her foot up the chimney. The giant's house is an ordinary house, but for the giant it's a doll's house. It's not that she's too big but that everything else is too small. However Alice, like Susan, is smart, and trusts her own good sense. Then there's Gulliver's second adventure in *Gulliver's Travels*, in which the hero finds himself in a land of giants. To the giantesses he's a plaything: they think he's a cute little fellow, and quite funny. What might it be like to look down on men, literally, instead of up to them? No doubt Susan has some insights.

And just remember: Whatever anyone tells you, size matters. And *Big Girls Don't Cry* counts the ways.

—MARGARET ATWOOD, February 15, 2024

BIG GIRLS DON'T CRY

Part One

I LIVED IN
THE GIANT'S HOUSE

1.

It's a hot day in early summer and I'm trying to hide my shameful body in the sand by the polliwog pond. The polliwogs have grown into fat squiggly black dots, with slender tails. They swim in funny, jerky motions across the pond, where dragonflies hover above water shimmering slimy and mysterious in the July sunshine. The polliwogs are metamorphosing into frogs and I'm metamorphosing too, although not in a good way.

The long skinny body that I'm covering with sand looks nothing like the film stars in the movie magazines of the 1950s. The skinny calves and knobby knees, the legs that grow and grow, the narrow hips and bony arms, the unruly curly hair. Not only is my body embarrassingly long, it's also embarrassingly thin. During the school year, I pad my clothes with extra sweaters and tops in an attempt to look like the petite curvaceous actresses I see in the Hollywood films.

Above and around me stretches my beach world. To the north, the long curve of sandy shoreline reaching to forested spits of land. And to the south, Poison Ivy Point with its secret sites like the dungeon staircase, a hidden path through scratchy juniper bushes, and the Hanging Step, an exposed tree root from which we gleefully jump into a sand dune. I've come up with those names because I'm the game maker, a role I play for the other children on the beach. They sit in front of our cottage waiting for me to think up things to cure their boredom on an endless summer day.

On this afternoon by the pond, none of these pleasures reassures me, although I'm cheerful by nature. Sunny, my husband calls me. Maybe. Taking an upbeat approach can also hide a myriad of fears. And that day, I'm struggling with a problem I can't fix. In just a few months I've grown a horrifying six inches. Only minutes before, my mother, Jane Swan, insisted on measuring me against the storeroom door of our cottage along with my friend who lives down the beach. My friend is tall, too, and in the last few months, she has grown a respectable one and a half inches; now she stands five foot nine. But I'm six foot two and I'm only twelve. My mother is also tall—she's five foot ten—and she often tells me to stop slouching. She doesn't understand that there's a world of difference between our heights, the same difference that exists between someone who is five foot two (short) and someone who is five foot six (average).

Like any kid, I have the usual challenges of schoolwork and sports competitions, and I tackle them by working hard. The measuring contest has presented me with something unfixable: I'm big.

Maybe, god forbid, I will get bigger.

THE WORD BIG is troublesome to me. It was then, and for many women and gender-fluid folk with feminine identities it still is. Being big is synonymous with being unfeminine. To be tall is to be big and to be big is to take up space, lots and lots of space—a cultural no-no for women of all sizes who are taught early on that they should take up less room, an echo of the days when Virginia Woolf said women's job was to reflect men back to themselves at twice life size.

And for that reason, many women, myself included, will unconsciously work to take up as little space as possible, deflecting compliments or swallowing their feelings to protect other people's egos. Even today, being feminine still means projecting a smaller public self, and women who do assert themselves are usually told they're too bossy, too dominant, too loud, and that they need to talk in a soft-spoken voice. Instead, we should all be encouraged to speak up, assert more, be bolder and more authoritative, and— here it comes—take up more space even if the cultural ideal is the shape of a girl's slender, unformed body. As a woman's body ages, her fuller breasts and rounded hips are often considered unsightly. So, for god's sake, whatever you do, stay skinny and don't take up too much room.

But everyone takes up space as they travel through their lives. Taking up space is how most of us learn who we are and what makes us happy. This is especially true for women, who are often taught to be smaller than their brothers and the boys they know, and, later on, smaller than their partners, or their husbands, or their colleagues. And if they become mothers, they may be expected to step aside and cede space to their children.

A FEW DAYS before that afternoon at the polliwog pond, a boy picked me up in his arms and tried to throw me into the lake.

She's too big for me, he announced when he fell down, taking me with him. How come she weighs so much? he asked my giggling friends as we struggled to our feet.

Your weight increases exponentially with every inch you grow—that's why. Tall women are "big" because they weigh more, so they aren't easily carried across a bridal threshold or swung up in a boy's arms like other girls. *Tall and big.* They go together. And being big, feeling big, is the sensation of overflowing what is designed for your fellow humans. It's the chair that doesn't quite fit or the table whose underside hits your knees at an uncomfortable angle.

When the measuring contest ended, I ran off to the polliwog pond and ignored my friend who was calling for me to come back. Until my mother marked down *six feet two inches* on the storeroom door, I had been able to fool myself into thinking I was the same height (more or less) as everyone else.

What a mistake! Guinness World Records, which celebrates the longest kiss and the heaviest onion, once defined a giantess as six foot two or more. So there you go. I'm a giant—a female one, to be sure. And that makes things worse.

2.

Before I became a giant, I lived in the giant's house. My six-foot-five father was a giant. His first name was Dalton, but everyone called him Doc Swan. When he stood in a doorway, he filled out the door frame almost entirely, tiny beams of light winking around his massive shoulders and torso.

Gigantic size brings back the experience of our childhoods, when huge monsters known as parents bossed us around. Think of Gulliver's fear of the giants he met in Jonathan Swift's book *Gulliver's Travels*. The sight of the giant farmwife's huge breast as she sat nursing her child terrified Gulliver, who had to shout to be heard by his hosts.

As befits a mythical person, my father is a remote figure. In my dreams, he roams through the rooms of our comfortable brick house in Midland, Ontario, like a distracted colossus. He hardly notices the chintz chairs and sofas purchased by my mother to replace the stiff Edwardian furniture that he used to own.

It's pitch-black in those dreams, the sun has set and there's the glimpse of a large body moving through space, and a sense of heaviness.

He doesn't want to turn on the lights and wake up my mother in our unlit house. He can't tell you what my mother's new furniture looks like, only that it's nice to sink his weary body into her sofa after a hard day at the office. He has memorized the placement of each piece as an object he needs to avoid when he goes out on a midnight call. He wears his dark Burberry winter coat with the big lapels; men's fashions then were styled to make them look big, as if he needed the extra inches.

I never see his face, only his turned-up collar and the massive plinth of his back, because he's getting ready to go out the door, his grey fedora settled comfortably on his large head, his mind already fixing on the three-car pileup at Angel's Corners and what carnage he will be obliged to repair. Severed heads, broken limbs, smashed-in faces with dangling eyeballs, a child run over by the wheel of a tractor-trailer. When the phone rings in the middle of

the night, he knows to expect the worst. Nobody calls at that hour
unless they are near death or dying.

He carries his black leather doctor's bag in case he needs to
operate on the side of the road. For a moment his bulk fills the
doorway like a second door, and then he's gone. There's the rum-
ble of his Chrysler Airflow starting up in the garage and then the
night is quiet again. *There is only work, work, work.*

3.

Despite his mythical stature, there was a hint that my remote father had a sense of humour. In the sunroom of our house he hung
the silly Dingbat calendar. It showed drawings of strange insect-
like creatures with wobbly balls on top of their antennas, performing weird-looking surgical procedures on other Dingbats, and I
imagined they were a version of my father operating on human
bodies. The Dingbats were small, fantastical creatures created
by the illustrator Dudley Ward. His popular cartoon characters
seemed mysteriously connected to my father's medical textbooks,
which were stacked in rows of shelves that rose to the ceiling of
our family library. My country-doctor father had the usual tomes,
such as *Gray's Anatomy*, first published in 1858, and scores of
other scholarly books with nubby red-leather covers.

Before the summer I grew to six foot two, these texts were a
premonition of things to come. One afternoon, I snuck into the
library and flipped through them. I never told anyone I found the
experience horrifying. They felt Gothic, unsettling—a window
into a part of being human that I preferred not to know about.

In my father's medical books, I saw graphic photographs of humans with genetic defects like a cleft palate and elephantiasis, with its abnormal swelling of arms and legs, and then there was the more frightening deformity of gigantism, the term for extreme height caused by a pituitary gland tumour that produces too much growth hormone. In some cases, this defect leads to the condition known as acromegaly, a widening of the giant's bones, which made the faces of some of the giants in the textbooks appear misshapen.

I was just beginning to understand what the impact of excessive size in my own life would be, but the cleft lip was already familiar because one of my schoolmates, Wayne, had one.

The roof of Wayne's mouth was visibly connected to his nose, distorting his face. People referred to Wayne's birth defect as a harelip, a term that would be considered an insult now. But in the 1950s, the people I grew up with in Midland assumed there was nothing wrong with commenting on physical infirmities, and they seemed blithely unaware of the possibility that someone's feelings might be hurt by their words.

Wayne was good-natured about insulting remarks, even when he stumbled over his words, and his voice sounded thick and slurred. He sat a row away from me in public school, and some days I would stare at his profile, wondering how he could stand it. This was the era before government health care in Canada, and Wayne's family couldn't afford the operation to get it fixed.

I secretly identified with Wayne. Like him, I possessed a body nobody else had. And you couldn't fix mine either. Or you could, but not easily.

4.

For many of us, our size is part of the way we pattern ourselves, and its influence affects us psychologically along with other markers such as our class background, our race, and our gender identities. The person who is very tall as a child and then grows into a short adult may continue to see themselves as tall, just as the very tall child who remains tall all their life will never forget the feeling of being seen as oversized.

Supermodels have made height glamorous in women, and the tendency to ridicule or disparage tall women isn't as common now as it used to be, although the former American First Lady Michelle Obama said in her book *The Light We Carry* that, given the neighbourhood she grew up in, her height was more of an issue than her skin colour. She explained that it's hard to know what we look like if we can't see ourselves reflected back by other people.

She wrote: "'Tall' became the label that got attached to me first, and it stuck with me right through. It was not something I could shake, not something I could hide about myself."

That afternoon by the pond, I'm burying myself in the sand, trying to do that very thing—hide. I've brought a pail and a sieve to catch the polliwogs and keep them in my aquarium at the cottage. But suddenly the idea seems childish and embarrassing, and I throw my kid's pail into the bushes, determined never to play with it again.

5.

My father took his strength for granted the way you do when you're big, without understanding that giants die young because their oversized bodies aren't designed to cope with gravity. And he believed every problem was solvable, if he was there to fix it. When a blizzard came up after tending to his Indigenous patients on what was known then as the Christian Island reserve, he found his way to the mainland by letting his terrier dog guide his horse and cutter across the ice. When a group of his friends were lost in the bush, he led them home. On a ship-to-shore radio during a November storm, he told a lighthouse keeper how to take out the appendix of the keeper's eight-year-old son. My father disarmed threatening drunks with a frowning look, and he was known for predicting to the day when a pregnant woman would have her baby. According to my mother, our father was the only person she knew who never had a crisis.

A tailor in Toronto made his huge three-piece suits along with his shirts, designed with extra-large pockets to contain his extra-large eyeglasses. His wing tips, size thirteen, were just the right length for the bodies of my smaller dolls. I would plunk them inside his long shoes, their rubber bodies splayed carelessly against the leather backs, their stiff hairdos hanging like golden frosting off their tiny heads.

Unbeknownst to him, I had seen him in the washroom without his pyjama bottoms, and the size of his penis shut down my imagination. I didn't know how any woman could receive such an extraordinary instrument. He seemed recklessly unaware of the power of his formidable body, dressing himself in civilian clothes and walking about like an ordinary human instead of the ogre in the "Jack and the Beanstalk" fairy tale.

Who can forget the one-eyed Cyclops who ate two of Odysseus's men in *The Odyssey*? Stories about my father's superhuman abilities abounded. It was said that he was as rich as King Midas because he'd made kazillions on the stock market. *False.* He lost his life savings during the crash of 1929 when a dishonest friend made off with his money and he had to rebuild his stock portfolio. It was the result, my mother said, of my father's trusting nature.

ONE NIGHT IN our Midland house, we're awakened by an eerie red light filling our bedroom windows. Firemen with hoses are rushing towards the public school across the road, and more fire trucks are arriving, their sirens wailing. The nuns who live nearby are trooping outside in single file. To my disappointment, they're still in their habits instead of wearing pyjamas, and they're watching the blaze in silent horror.

My mother stands between me and my brother, John, her arms on our shoulders. She's trembling.

In the master bedroom, my father lies snoring while the roar of the fire grows louder and louder. My mother sends my brother to rouse him. He comes a few minutes later in his rumpled pyjamas, yawning and looking unconcerned. When I shriek at the sight of sparks landing on the cedar hedge by our driveway, he says: It rained earlier. The cedars won't catch fire.

He's looking at me when he speaks. A first. He almost never looks at me on his Sunday calls to the farms around Midland, on the occasions when he takes our family with him as a special treat. Usually he just stares right through me. Maybe he's thinking about a housewife dying of cancer or a farmer falling into his threshing machine. His weary, glassy-eyed stare makes me feel spacey and disconnected, as if I'm not real. Maybe he thought I wasn't worth his attention. Or maybe his perception was the truth: maybe I didn't exist to him, a frightening thought.

But he sees me now. I can feel it. He squeezes my arm and I'm reassured. Several years ago, I pretended to be sick in order to get his attention, and he gave me a candy with a distracted nod and turned back to his work.

He glances one more time at the fire, still looking unperturbed, and then he stumbles back to the master bedroom, where he begins to snore again. My mother seems uncertain. I sense the wheel of her thoughts turning. Perhaps she should wake him a second time and insist he take control of the situation. Or perhaps we should leave him be, gather up our belongings and run for our lives . . .

As we stand wondering what to do, the flames, which only moments before seemed to lick the roof of the sky, those terrifying flames are growing noticeably smaller. Most of the building has been consumed, and we can see the metal frames of the floors glowing through the fallen timbers. Relieved to be out of danger, we watch the blaze die down in the same way campers stare contentedly at the embers of a bonfire.

The fire burns itself out, and we go back to bed. The next morning, the Midland radio station says no one has been harmed. My mother was right when she said our father was unflappable. His formidable size likely had everything to do with it.

6.

The life of an adolescent is often rife with humiliating experiences. Here are some of mine:

Children laughed at me on the street. A short teenage boy made his friends crack up by saying it would be a biological impossibility to have a child with me. (He didn't know much about sex. But then neither did I. We didn't know we were all the same height lying down.) The eyes of another teenage boy filled with tears when he realized I was his blind date. He also developed a headache. A girlfriend at a sock hop told me no boy wanted to embarrass himself by dancing with me. Why? I was too tall. In a sneering tone, another boy said he asked me out because he knew a girl my size would be grateful for his attention. Strangers asked if I played basketball, hardy har har. I would say no, although of course I did. Isn't it too bad you're a girl when you're so tall, the mothers of my friends liked to coo, failing to understand that it felt like they were wishing me a life of rejection.

I was fourteen when the boy who became my first husband told me about a magazine article on the Nova Scotia giantess Anna Swan. She lived from 1846 to 1888, and exhibited with P.T. Barnum. Maybe you'll join the circus too, he joked before suggesting I get four inches cut off my thighbones so I wouldn't be a freak like her.

His remark terrified me even though Anna was seven foot six and weighed 418 pounds and her family was *not* related to mine. Nor did I suffer from a pituitary tumour, which is what had caused her extraordinary height.

Nevertheless, from that day on, I prayed no one would find out about Anna Swan. The thought of growing up to become a giantess filled me with horror. What if my family really was related to hers, and I grew another seven or eight inches? Was that what adult life held in store?

A SCENE FROM *the memory bank:*

I'm sitting alone in the murky light of a friend's rec room, watching my grade-six friends jive, kid-style, to "Rock Around the Clock" by Bill Haley. I love jiving, but nobody asks me to dance even though I'm decked out in my favourite outfit, a stiff green-felt skirt decorated with poodle decals and a blouse with a Peter Pan collar. I belong to a grade-six clique called the "Hi-Fi Club," so named for the popular 1950s hi-fi record players with turntables. I'm still sitting by myself when "Whole Lotta Shakin' Goin' On" by Little Richard is put on the record player. One of the other girls shimmies her shoulders as she dances by me and announces: The boys aren't asking Susan to dance because she's too tall.

Did she really say that? She did. I can still feel the sting of her words as she delivers the bad news: *Nobody wants you for a partner.* Before she pointed this out, I didn't think of myself as undesirable. From that moment on, I avoided looking at photographs that depicted me towering over my schoolmates. Later, when my daughter became a tall teenager, I wrote out a list of snappy comebacks like, *Yes, I'm over six feet. What's your problem?* Armed with such one-liners, she never complained about her height again. But in the 1950s I had no idea how to react to nasty put-downs about my size. Except to feel humiliated, which is the reaction many people have when their body doesn't look like the bodies of other people.

My mother worried about the impact of the nasty put-downs on me and on my brother, John, who was a broad-shouldered boy well over six feet. John had been going through a difficult time with his hockey coach, a Presbyterian minister, no less, who insisted John rough up the boys on the other team. My mother ordered John to ignore him. She said he needed to learn self-restraint so he wouldn't be seen as a bully. He obeyed my mother, not his coach, and learned to defuse confrontations with shorter boys who often attacked him to prove their masculinity. At a bonfire, three boys once jumped on John's back and tried to wrestle him to the ground. With the boys clinging to his neck and shoulders, he walked into the lake and shook them off the way a dog sheds fleas. Like our father, he had learned how to de-escalate conflict.

He grew up to be six foot eight, and later, after he became a real estate agent, he built his own giant's house, which features a long, long, one-storey flight of stairs six feet across. That's almost double the standard width of construction codes. Walking down that enormous staircase evokes the sensation of descending the stairs of a public monument.

Boxes, boxes everywhere

In my brother's life and mine, being big has always been something to contend with.

It's not just a matter of finding clothes and shoes. Doctors and dentists don't give you enough anesthetic. You have to writhe in discomfort before they up the dose of painkiller. When I broke my elbow, a medical team gave me too little anesthetic and I could feel the pinch of the surgeon's knife, so the operation had to be stopped.

Both my brother and I are known in our family for leaving jars half-open and ripping the tops off of cereal boxes, as if a package of granola is an obstacle made to test the patience of someone with very long fingers. My husband likes to joke about opening a cupboard and having a container of rice fall onto his head, or shaking a bottle of orange juice before pouring himself a glass only to have the liquid spill all over his shirt because the top wasn't screwed on properly. Giants have a problem with material reality; we lurch and blunder about because the physical world doesn't fit us the way it does most humans.

It's the taking up space issue again. Which brings me to boxes: the boxes that we place ourselves in and the boxes other people are placed in by our society. These boxes are social, political, cultural, or psychological constructions, and they are everywhere you look, often limiting our ability to be our best selves.

Every person needs a framework in order to grow, but why are we forced into boxes that keep us from developing our abilities? Isn't becoming an adult about finding out who we want to be as we live and breathe in the real dimensions of time and space?

Everybody has boxes, and here are some of mine.

The smaller-bedroom box

As a girl, I was given the smallest bedroom in our Midland house. John, who was two years younger and physically smaller then, was given the larger bedroom. I prided myself on accepting the smaller bedroom without complaining, and when, years later, my mother thought it was my turn and offered me the big bedroom, I was too proud to accept. Instead, I huffily declined and said I liked my small bedroom. It's got a better view and a nicer bed, and besides, it's mine. (And good for me for coming up with a strategy to protect my self-esteem when somebody considers me lesser.)

Then, years and years later, in a country house I rented with my brother and my husband, I remember thinking, *It's time for me to have the big bedroom now*. It only took me seventy-eight years to feel comfortable saying that to myself.

Why is it so easy to give up space when you're a woman? Because others expect it and we expect it of ourselves? Is that why so many of us work hard at making ourselves small?

Granted, a boy relegated to the less appealing bedroom could pride himself on having it for the same reasons I did, but it's usually girls who are given (and accept) the smaller space.

The physical dimensions of a bedroom make it easy to imagine a box. The height of its ceiling, the span of its floor. Are there large modern windows, or are the windows tiny, the way they are in nineteenth-century houses? And will you be like Alice in the White Rabbit's house as she sticks an arm out the window and her foot up the chimney and cries in exasperation, "I can do no more. . . . What will become of me?" How can you stretch to your full size in spaces no bigger than a prison cell? Maybe it's better not to stretch at all. Or so the reasoning can go.

Why not come out and say what I'm thinking? It's not only about physical spaces. The boxes that concern me most are psychological.

The go-along box

When you're in a box and it doesn't fit (and sometimes even if it does), you struggle to get out of it. Few people want to live inside a box that others have created for them, although there's no escaping the fact that your first box will be something others have created and you won't have much choice in the matter. It will be the crib or the bassinet and the home you grew up in and the space outside that home.

I didn't understand the nature of the box I lived in until I was ten, but before I go back to that experience, I should explain that my town, Midland, Ontario, on the shores of Georgian Bay, was the home of just over eight thousand people, and it was economically depressed.

It started as a prosperous nineteenth-century railroad depot, transporting grain and lumber to the cities. When I lived there in the 1950s, those days were over, and the town's prosperity hadn't returned despite new factories that made cameras and ball gowns. Poverty was an issue for many white farmers and the Indigenous community on the reserve on Christian Island. Some families had to ration bites of a single potato to their children, while families like mine, whose fathers were teachers or doctors, lived more comfortably.

The tourist industry was a partial solution to Midland's economic troubles, and visitors came every summer from all over Canada and the United States to cottages on the beautiful stretch of pine and rock islands on eastern Georgian Bay. Holy moly, they're back *touristing* again, our babysitter liked to complain, forgetting that our summer visitors went home in September, leaving Midland in the same doldrums as before.

A somber Presbyterian mood dominated. Most of the large stolid brick homes had belonged to lumber barons or ship captains, and a post-pioneer gentility prevailed on both sides of the hills on which Midland was built. My father's office was on the main street, which ran down the valley between these hills like a long sloping ski trail leading to the Midland harbour, where cruise ships and freighters carrying grain docked regularly.

Given the town's poor economic circumstances, my father was often paid in cabbages and chickens. His work as a doctor defined our family. Mothers of my friends regularly cleaned their homes before I visited because I was his daughter. Which brings me to the birthday party of my French-Canadian friend, a ten-year-old classmate who lived on what was called the wrong side of town. A man named John Dollar had built a sawmill there years ago, and that poor section of Midland was referred to as Dollar Town (no irony intended). My father liked to joke about Dollar Town steaks, which had nothing to do with steaks. The term meant fried pieces of baloney.

IT'S A COOL night in October. Halloween is coming, and to get to my friend's house, I need to walk by a thickly wooded area where the fall wind is moaning through the branches of the maples, whose leaves are turning crimson and lemon yellow. Only weeks before, a deadly rabies virus had infected wild animals and put the town on alert. There were stories of rabid coyotes with foaming mouths attacking people and dogs on the street. As I walk past the woods, I hear a rustling noise coming from the bushes. I'm convinced it's a rabid wolf and it's following me, creeping closer and closer.

In a panic, I start running towards the street my classmate lives on, clutching my birthday present. I haven't been to her house before so I don't know she lives in a tarpaper shack. The sight shocks me out of my anxious imaginings. The noise I thought was a wolf is the rustling of the tissue paper wrapped around her birthday present.

Feeling foolish, I go inside. My friend rushes over to say hello and I'm too surprised to speak. There's almost no furniture. Just a few broken-down kitchen chairs placed around a shabby-looking table. Its top is covered in checkered grey linoleum. A lopsided chocolate cake sits on the table and an old-fashioned hand pump stands by the washbasin; the sole heat appears to be coming from a woodstove. Her mother is nervous when she greets me and, sure enough, she says she has just washed the kitchen floor because she knew Doc Swan's daughter was coming.

Her clean floor was likely a show of respect for my father. She probably did it for the minister too. But I'm ashamed that someone like her had to spend time cleaning her house for a kid like me. As I stand listening, my mind spins with questions. It's my first experience with understanding privilege. Why am I lucky and my friend is not? And how much do the lucky ones like me get to keep for ourselves and how much should we give away? (The question haunts me still.) Some sacrifice is needed when the scales are not balanced. But what should I sacrifice? Is penance required?

After the party, my mother picks me up in our car because it's late and the Midland streets are dark. When I tell her about my experience, she says that people who live in tarpaper shacks like my friend whose father works in the planing mill do so because they aren't as smart as people who have professional jobs in law and medicine.

It's more complicated than that, I know. In a small town, class difference is easy to see. The people with money and a nice home live side by side with those who don't, and in many cases, it's not clear why some are rich and others are not.

Although I disagree with her, I sit listening quietly. Her opinion about social hierarchies can't be shaken. On a Caribbean holiday that year, she told me not to bother making friends with the kind Bahamian teenager who ran the elevator because he would be the maître d' when I returned later with my husband. I didn't think his fate was predetermined, and I didn't see myself returning to the resort as a version of my mother with a husband on my arm. I was determined to be a writer, and husbands and children weren't going to be my first priority. But what was the point of arguing with her? Besides, she often chided me for posing embarrassing questions, like the time I asked our Anglican minister if Jesus was a cult leader.

On a cold afternoon in March, the spring sunlight is firing up the stained-glass window behind his head as he sits in the church vestry talking to me about the catechism in my confirmation ceremony. He drones on and on until I pipe up and say, Sir, I have a question. Before he can refuse me, I ask how he knows that Jesus wasn't crazy and prone to hallucinations. I used the word *crazy* because that's how we talked in the fifties, but I was careful not to speak in a smart-alecky tone that might suggest I was being disrespectful. I was guileless then and, in many ways, I'm guileless still. I just want to know why a minister like him thinks Jesus was on the up and up. Is that a crime?

Our Anglican minister is a thin man with papery white skin and a whispery voice. His face radiates a glimmer of saintliness as he clasps and re-clasps his hands, straining to understand but frightened I might say something even more outlandish and reprehensible, and he'll have no answer except to say it's time for him to go back to the manse, where his wife is cooking dinner. I stumble over my words, doing my best to show him I don't mean to be obnoxious. Other than the Bible, I politely point out, there's no factual evidence about Jesus, so why do we believe what the Bible says? Weren't the accounts about Jesus written a century or two after the Son of God lived?

Christians need to accept what the Bible tells us, he replies. But why, I persist. Silence. He could have mentioned that some scholars were starting to question whether stories in the Bible were meant to convey the meaning of events, and that historical accuracy wasn't their concern, but it was the fifties, when Protestant churches were unable to admit there might be different interpretations of Christian doctrine. Clearing his throat, he gets up from his desk, making it clear our meeting is over. I thank him and leave. In a small Ontario town in that era, there's no use persevering with difficult questions. It's better to go along.

But questions are useful. Questions are the key to getting out of uncomfortable boxes, boxes in which I find myself, squirming and wriggling so I can move with ease instead of rolling myself up into a ball in order to fit. Questions like, What can I do to make this box feel comfortable? Or, Why am I unhappy when this box is supposed to have everything I want? Boxes and questions—they go together from the start to the end of our lives.

If you'd asked me during my childhood about my hunger for answers, a need that would go hand in hand with my skepticism as an adult, I wouldn't have had a clue what you were talking about. My size was the issue, and it was already attracting too much attention. *Help, I'm in a runaway body* was the sensation I experienced as a girl. I sensed without really understanding why that people considered a big female body threatening, and even dangerous.

The poster for the 1958 movie *Attack of the 50 Foot Woman* says it all. She's a beautiful, long-haired giantess dressed in a skimpy outfit and she goes on a rampage, plucking cars with shark fins from a highway overpass as if they were toys because she's taking revenge on an unfaithful husband. The giantess, played by Allison Hayes, can squash men like bugs, and it's obvious now in a way it wasn't to me as a girl that she's a metaphor for the fear that men can feel about women who dare to make demands and take up space.

The giantess in *Attack of the 50 Foot Woman* dies tragically after the local sheriff fires a shotgun at her, causing a power line transformer to blow up and kill her.

In the 2019 movie *Tall Girl*, an insecure six-foot-one-and-a-half-inch-tall girl played by Ava Michelle is luckier. She slowly learns to accept herself, and the movie ends sweetly with the short boy who is crazy about her standing on a milk crate in order to kiss her.

My growth spurt worried my parents. They took me to a To-ronto endocrinologist to see if it could be slowed or stopped. The endocrinologist, who specialized in growth hormones, recom-mended they do nothing because my growth cycle was almost finished, and my parents agreed. My father had never liked the idea of playing with my physical chemistry anyway.

I barely remember the visit. My parents were careful not to stress my size. Afterwards, my mother took me to the tall girls' shop called Rowena's, and I hated the dowdy clothes she bought for me that day. I preferred the dresses and pants you could buy from regular clothing stores, even if their outfits looked like they had shrunk in the wash when I put them on. In time, I came to prefer the shrunk look. A blouse that fit me—that is, a blouse with sleeves that came to my wrists—appeared oversized and ungainly to my critical eyes.

At the end of the summer, my parents sent me away to board-ing school to avoid the pressures of a co-ed high school, with its popularity contests and habit of calling kids with good marks brown-nosers or sucks. At Havergal College, my above-average grades were admired, and later I would become a prefect in a weepy spring rite when girls tied knots in my tasseled belt. I also played on all the athletic teams, including basketball. Before games, I was encouraged to walk around the court to intimidate the other team. During one match the forward I was guarding broke down and sobbed because she couldn't score with me blocking her shots. Afterwards, our coach complimented me and so did the other girls.

Were they jealous of my prowess? You must be joking. It was the early sixties. No girl wanted to be my height.

The spinster box

When I was twenty-six and learning how to write fiction, I was sitting at my glass table in the front room of a Toronto house when a ghost from my past walked by my window. She wasn't really a ghost, although I thought of Catherine Steele that way because I was working hard at pretending I hadn't attended an elite boarding school for girls. She had been our headmistress. Her nickname was Stainless Steele, and she was the freethinking daughter of an old Toronto family that had started a prosperous seeds company. Their massive brick warehouse, which once had a private railcar siding, still stands on a downtown street.

Catherine Steele didn't marry at a time when women were expected to become wives and mothers. Instead, she did graduate work in sociology at Columbia University in New York City in the 1930s. Sociology was considered a radical subject then. Her degree qualified her to teach at a university but the job she found was heading up a girls' school.

She was almost six foot two like me and ungainly, with bloodhound eyes. She wore her thin grey hair curled in a tight, unflattering roll across the nape of her neck, and when she walked down the corridors of my girls' school during study halls, the sound of her feet in her ugly round-toed shoes echoed like drum beats on the parquet floors, sending the girls in the classrooms into a frenzy. They would start pounding their desks in imitation of the dreaded sound.

The desk-pounding was a warning: *Stainless is out for blood. Quit whispering—get rid of your chewing gum. Put away that nail polish unless you want an orderly mark.*

AT SCHOOL, I'M shy and, ordinarily, I go out of my way to avoid serious trouble.

But this is different. *So different.* Stainless is known to like me, and being favoured by a headmistress who terrifies my classmates will go against me. So, I don't stop chewing gum or putting on Tropical Dawn nail polish. Slowly and methodically, I keep at the nail polishing until I hear the loud rap-rap-rap and look up to see her face. Her bloodhound eyes appear large and terrifying in the window of the classroom door. She points a witchy finger at my nail polish bottle and beckons. Head down, I struggle to my feet while the other girls utter frightened little gasps. I'm aware I should be terrified, but all I feel is light-headed, even giddy.

Thank my lucky stars I'm in trouble again. It's another victory for girls like myself in our private war against spinsters. The skirmishes are spearheaded by Stainless Steele, who runs the boarding school like an army, issuing punishments right and left. Our enemy judges us guilty until proven innocent, and five detentions results in an orderly mark that suspends your right to visit friends on the weekend. No personal possessions are allowed on our dresser tops. No posters on the wall or clothes left on our chairs. We line up for inspection of our bedrooms every morning while the matrons check to see if the hems of our uniforms come to our knees and whether we have tucked in the hospital corners properly on our beds. We sleep in narrow cots with brown utilitarian bedspreads.

With its constant bells and rules, the boarding school is an ideal atmosphere for my own tiny rebellions, like stealing cookies from the night table while our matron Mrs. Hansen isn't looking, and twirling around in my dressing gown to show off its bulging pockets, waiting for her to shriek in her Norwegian accent, her teeth clacking like the Charlie McCarthy dummy: Vesen Vaan, you have a detention! (Good!) Or peeing into a glass of water when I'm forbidden to use the washroom after lights out (even better), defiantly leaving the glass of urine on the windowsill overnight (Take that, I dare you!), and returning from breakfast the next morning to find the glass has disappeared, without the matron giving me another black mark. Was my behaviour too unspeakable to mention? (Worse luck.)

Once we're in her office, Stainless closes the door. Smiling warmly, she begins to scold me about getting detentions for something as silly as chewing gum and putting on nail polish during study hours. I agree, although she doesn't know I keep a running tab of black marks so nobody can accuse me of being her pet. She has told me several times that I have good character and that's why she insists I room with girls who she thinks need to be brought out of their shells. Grudgingly I go along, although it means I rarely get to room with my friends.

Soon she is talking to me (like she always does on these occasions) about the books she's reading and the difference between the work of Charlotte Brontë and Jane Austen. She prefers Brontë. More open fields, Stainless says, a bigger vista. I can't stop myself from nodding, and in no time, I find myself telling her why *Jane Eyre* is the best novel I've ever read.

I'm aware that I'm sitting there enjoying myself with that ridiculed figure, a spinster, who refuses to cater to men and who allows only three of them inside the school on a regular basis: Reverend Dan, the lanky Anglican minister whose boyish good looks cause some girls to develop crushes; and the night janitor, an East European immigrant whose name I don't know because he works while we sleep. He's a former architect who should by rights have a better job. Finally, there's Stefan, the wacky daytime janitor who giggles and winks at us as he drags around a huge and embarrassing cardboard Kotex box in the school halls, looking for garbage to throw into it.

What does someone like Stainless know about the outside world of men? Or boys, for that matter, who aren't allowed inside the school except on special occasions like the Boarders Dance?

AN ALL-GIRLS' SCHOOL is a refuge for someone my size. However, the Boarders Dance reminds me all too well that beyond our school gates the real world with its cruel expectations waits.

Imagine me (imagine us) on a gloomy fall night in the land of the spinsters, fourteen, fifteen years old, waiting anxiously with the other girls as dozens of teenage boys file from their school bus into our school lobby. Imagine that only a few days before, Elvis Presley made his groundbreaking appearance on the Ed Sullivan television show, his sultry combo of gospel music and rhythm and blues bringing a Black version of rock and roll to white teenagers like us.

Imagine some boys with slicked-back hair in an Elvis-style ducktail, others sporting brush cuts and conservative sports jackets—not your typical group of gawky adolescents but boarders at an elite Toronto school that has the late Prince Philip as a patron.

Imagine the girls in puffy dresses with crinolines, and bouffant hairdos, me in a baggy puce-coloured sack dress that I mistakenly think is sophisticated. Imagine my curly fair hair sticky with hair-spray, my pair of black-patent leather flats in lieu of high heels because I'm tall.

We're about to undergo the horrors of the Boarders Dance, the mass blind date for kids from grades nine and ten, unaware that the staff at both our schools has matched up the girls and boys without bothering to check their heights.

A matron calls my name and the name of a boy. In the style of animals boarding Noah's ark, we stumble into the middle of the room. Giggles break out.

A squib of a boy, with coke-bottle glasses, looks up at me in shock. He must be five foot four.

Together we walk into the auditorium, where a few hours ear-lier the other girls and I had enthusiastically strewn the walls with sausage-shaped balloons and red and black crepe. The hit song "Blue Moon" reverberates through the room as the boy fumbles for my hand. Reluctantly, we start to slow dance, the top of his head no higher than my chin. He has smeared Clearasil on his forehead to cover his pimples and I can smell a pungent sweaty odour under his Old Spice deodorant. Ugh, his hands are wet. He's perspiring heavily and he drops my hand in case I'm repulsed. I am repulsed. Luckily, "Cathy's Clown" by the Everly Brothers comes on, and we weave and bob to the faster tune, dancing far apart, gyrating vaguely in each other's direction so nobody will think we're a couple.

In a worried voice, he tells me he has to sit down. He has a headache. I offer to find some aspirins for him. He barely responds, and off I go acting out a parody of the Good Samaritan. My Midland classmate Wayne would be proud of the good-natured person I'm trying to be. On my return, I find my blind date sitting on a bleacher, holding his head in his palms, his eyes shiny with tears. I feel a stab of horror: I'm the cause of his distress.

I don't know how either of us got through the night.

ON THE STREET in front of my Toronto house, Catherine Steele had stopped walking. She was looking directly at me through my living room window. I sat very still, hoping her X-ray eyes wouldn't spot me behind my desk. As she stared, my old guilty feelings came rushing back along with the memory of my first day at boarding school. So here I go, down into the rabbit hole of my past . . .

Above the school's concrete steps, the Gothic tower rises like the turret of a fairy-tale castle. Up, up it goes into the cloudless September sky. It strains my neck to look. My grandmother and my father hover nearby. My mother is sick that day, and, surprisingly, he's able to put aside his work and take me to school.

My father clutches my arm as if something big and fearful is about to happen, and that's not far from the truth. I'll be without my parents for the first time, cooped up like a prisoner in an all-girls' institution where I'll be allowed home only twice before Christmas and only once after that holiday.

He and I go inside the school, my large, broad-shouldered father looking out of place in its cavernous lobby. He is, after all, a man, and men rarely pass without permission through these heavy doors with the tiny twinkly glass windows.

The vice-principal, as round as a Toby jug, steps out of the shadows. She shakes my father's hand, looking over at me with friendly sympathy. She knows I'm about to experience the life of a full-time boarder, which will bring intimate knowledge of the school's quaint ways: the cliques of snooty day girls, the constant bell-ringing, the interminable halls that reek of floor wax, and, most important, the eccentric teachers and professors who rule our lives. When I write my novel *The Wives of Bath*, it won't be hard to create teachers like Miss Muckle, who taught English, and Miss Dyke, who taught history. (Yes, those were really their names.) These strong, eccentric women will go down on the page as I remember them.

Calm down, I tell myself. *That was years ago, and you're sitting at your desk writing a short story.* But I'm not calm. I'm confused and rattled. Of course, Stainless sees me. She hasn't moved since I first saw her, and she's still looking directly at me through my living room window, waiting politely for me to acknowledge her and invite her into my home. I continue to sit motionless, as if I don't know she's there, and wait for her to go. A moment later she pulls her coat more tightly about her and strides off. She still wears the same ugly gunboats on her feet, although she appears to be moving more slowly than I remember. Is it my imagination or do her shoulders look a little more stooped?

I haven't seen her for a decade, and everything about that time felt different. For one thing, women who took jobs outside the home were looked down on, and many of our teachers and matrons were likely there because they badly needed the money. Most of them were widows or had husbands who had mysteriously disappeared, but as far as I was concerned—in my girlish ignorance—they were still forsaken spinsters, even if they stuck *Mrs.* in front of their names. It was whispered that some of our teachers loved women, and the word *lesbian* led to lots of anxious joking about the dangers of being "a les," without any of us having the faintest idea of what being a lesbian meant.

Nineteen sixty-three was the year President Kennedy was shot and Martin Luther King Jr. gave his famous "I have a dream" speech. That fall, during my last year in boarding school, my father died and Stainless brought my classmates up to Midland for his funeral. It was a sad, solemn affair with over one thousand mourners packed into the small Anglican church one block from our house. It was said that hard work killed him, but no autopsy had been performed so we didn't know for sure.

At the cemetery, her head sticks up above the shoulders of the other mourners, her large hound dog eyes glowing beneath a hat trimmed with pheasants' feathers. She senses me staring, and her eyes soften. She looks sympathetic, as if she knows my father has died just when I'm at the stage of my life when I need his love and reassurance most. And that after his extra-large coffin vanishes into the earth, some part of me will feel unacknowledged forever.

When the graveside service ends, I don't go over and say how much I appreciate her coming with my schoolmates. It's a cold December day and I hurry home with my mother. I know why I snubbed her at my father's funeral, but why did I ignore her the day she appeared on my Toronto street? Why didn't I get up and invite her in? As I write this, I'm sitting at the same modern glass table I used then. I've brought the table, with its still-stylish but tarnished brass legs, out from the laundry room because I'm changing my workstation, and here I sit with pages of manuscript sprawled over its glass surface. I've come full circle. Would I turn my headmistress away if she showed up at my door today? *Of course not.* And would I still be angry because she insisted I room with girls who had problems? *Hardly.* One of those roommates became my best friend. And surely as a young woman I no longer cared if my schoolmates knew Stainless liked me. Then why had I been so determined *not* to be friendly the day she appeared in front of my house? The answer hits with a thud. Absurd as it sounds, I was still nervous about the possibility of social contagion, as if being nice to her would lead me to adopt spinsterish ways and I would end up the loveless woman I naively imagined her to be, obliged to work at a job below my abilities inside a patriarchal universe that would never appreciate my worth. So there was no way I would accept her overtures of friendship, and when she strode off down the street I turned back to my writing and shut her out of my thoughts.

NOT LONG AFTER I saw my headmistress on the Toronto street, I dreamt about a woman with a colossal stone head. In the dream, a tiny woman was opening the top of the skull of the giant woman like a submarine hatch. A ladder had been placed against the statue so she could climb down. I didn't understand the dream at the time, but it likely refers to my habit of not fitting, and how I tried hard to adapt only to end up struggling with the styles of womanhood passed on by the mentoring figures of my girlhood—like my headmistress, Catherine Steele, and the women in my family. What were their feminine styles but more boxes that didn't fit, boxes that I needed to burst out of so I could be myself?

The dutiful-daughter box

During the summers when I was in my late twenties and learning to write fiction, I sometimes stayed with my mother in her summer home, a log cabin on Lake Huron, and in the mornings, I'd bike the mile and a half to my grandmother's house in Sarnia in order to write. My mother had encouraged my writing since I was a child. My grandmother Pauline Cowan wasn't as interested in my stories, but she let me use her attic as my office. It was a quiet space far above her substantial duplex, which included a rented apartment on the second floor and my grandmother's quarters on the first.

I wrote in the morning, only stopping for an hour for lunch at noon when my grandmother's maid, Georgette, set out plates of tuna fish sandwiches and ginger ale on my grandmother's Sheraton dining table. My grandmother ate with me, sipping "her gin and anything," as she put it, and when she wanted Georgette to take our plates away, she pressed her foot on the buzzer beneath the table, and Georgette would rush back in, her high sweet voice trilling with enthusiasm over the weather or something my grandmother did, giggling and praising my grandmother's silky white hair, and insisting she would look like such a beautiful doll in her coffin.

Georgette was a French-Canadian Catholic who took her religion far more seriously than my family took our Anglican faith,

and how you looked at your own funeral was important. She had
short frizzy brown hair whose curls appeared frozen to her head.
It was hard to say how she achieved that effect, but whatever
product she used was more formidable than mere hairspray. Her
mouth was usually open in a broad, good-natured smile, exposing
an unfortunate set of false teeth that made the lower part of her
face look horsey.

ONE AFTERNOON IN August, while I was writing, I heard
the plaintive voice of my grandmother, and I went to the attic
window to see what was wrong. After lunch, she usually sat in
her garden in her lawn chair, with her cat Baby on her lap, wearing her thick Coke-bottle glasses that were a result of a misman-
aged cataract operation. She liked to poke at the nearby petunia
plot with her cane, as if she was protesting her poor eyesight and
failing health. This afternoon, my mother, Jane, was sitting next
to her, and the two of them presented a troubling tableau. My
mother was a beautiful, fair-haired woman who wasn't interested
in another husband because she was enjoying the independence
of being a widow. And that day, her lovely face was a mask of
unexpressed exasperation. She was likely listening to one of my
grandmother's tirades about how my mother needed to get married again. My grandmother had a family friend in mind, a retired
insurance salesman and local windbag who showed up uninvited
at my mother's log cabin looking for a cup of coffee. My mother
couldn't stand him, and my grandmother didn't think much of
him either, but she was determined that my mother remarry because she thought women needed husbands to look after them.

After my grandfather died, she had married again at seventy-five to Brownie Lamason, an old boyfriend she hadn't seen for fifty years, and they had been very happy until his death at eighty-six, the age my grandmother was that morning.

My mother had no intention of remarrying, although she didn't tell my grandmother that. My grandmother had taught her children that contradicting people and refusing their requests might hurt their feelings, especially my grandmother's feelings if my mother didn't do what my grandmother wanted. It was part of haute WASP etiquette, and most of my family went along with my grandmother's unspoken rule: you shouldn't ask anybody for anything directly—you had to do it by performing little courtesies and considerations that could end up getting you what you wanted.

That afternoon, Georgette came out with a tea tray and set it down on a black wrought-iron table beside my grandmother. She had on the white uniform that my grandmother made her wear and its colour glistened like snow in the scorching August sunlight. Her mouth kept opening and closing as if she was trying to talk to my grandmother, but my grandmother wasn't paying attention. Her attention was on my mother, her favourite child, and when she noticed Georgette still standing there, she said something and waved her away. I wondered if she had made a nasty remark, because Georgette hurried back to the house, her head down, and my mother and grandmother continued to talk, their faces glum. As I watched, a feeling of hopelessness and frustration came over me. If I were to take a psychological test, chances are I would be classified as a first responder who rushes in to help at the first sign of trouble. More than once, I've been told I'm like the catcher in the rye mentioned by Holden Caulfield, the fictional character in J.D. Salinger's famous novel, who wants to save children from falling off a cliff. However, in my case, the first-responder reaction can happen without me bothering to check whether the person really needs help. And although I didn't know it at the time, my mother and grandmother were teaching me two important lessons; namely, that it was impossible to help people who don't want to be helped and that I needed to assess each situation carefully before I reacted.

I began pacing back and forth in the attic room, longing for my mother to free herself from my grandmother's demands. Like many mothers and daughters in families such as mine, they didn't know how to communicate their needs to each other, and that failure created a pattern of emotional turmoil that meant nothing was going to change.

But that afternoon, Georgette would change everything when she tried to attack my grandmother with her own kitchen knife. Let me save for a moment that excruciating story while I give you some background on my mother and grandmother, because finding enough space for yourself in the dutiful-daughter box is like walking through a maze in a formal garden where women's paths are so intertwined you can't tell where your mother's path ends and your own path begins. And the differences between my mother and grandmother were confounding.

MY GRANDMOTHER WAS the matriarch of the family, and she dominated us through her confidence and charm and the family money that she had inherited from her father, the lawyer

Frederick Pardee, who was the parliamentary whip for Canadian prime minister Wilfrid Laurier. Then there was her grandfather Timothy Blair Pardee, whose feminist views existed in the constellation of our relatives like a distant planet whose faint starlight reached us over a century of time.

Like his son, Timothy Pardee had been a lawyer and a politician. In the late nineteenth century, he went against his party and the clergy and won the right for women to work in government buildings. He was a good friend of Walt Whitman, the American poet who came up to Canada to play cards with my great-great-grandfather and the psychiatrist Richard Maurice Bucke. Bucke ran the psychiatric hospital in London, Ontario, where he introduced a new policy of humane treatment for patients. He also wrote *Cosmic Consciousness*. Published in 1901, this non-fiction book has never been out of print.

When Walt Whitman came to town, the women in our family shook their heads in dread. Whitman's visits meant anarchy was set loose in their Victorian household. The men stayed up all night playing cards and talking philosophy. Meals wouldn't happen on their usual schedule; beds would be left unmade because the American poet, who had travelled all the way from Camden, New Jersey, to see his friends, didn't get up at regular hours. There was no predicting what could happen. Perhaps the men would indulge in nude sunbathing on their swimming picnics, because Whitman believed nude sunbathing was good for your health.

As if this patrician background wasn't enough, the money my grandmother inherited from her senator father gave her a power that the other women in my family lacked, and she didn't feel ashamed or embarrassed like I did about being privileged. The

contemporary use of the word *privilege* would baffle her. She gave
food to the homeless men who showed up at her door in the 1930s
and then off she went to her parties and tennis games without
thinking anything more about it. There are family photographs of
my grandmother and mother dressed in jodhpurs and high boots,
riding horses during the Great Depression. Their horses were kept
in a barn on acres of sprawling family property near Lake Huron,
and she and my grandfather travelled by private railway car to visit
friends in faraway places like California.

I have a colour photograph of her in the backyard of her Vidal
Street house in Sarnia. She's upholding her reputation as a twenties flapper by drinking gin with the minister and some male
friends after a church service. A flowered hat sits on her head, and
a reddish-brown fur scarf made from the bodies of stone martens
has been draped across her broad shoulders. The gruesome sight
of their tiny dead faces used to make me shiver.

In the photo, my grandmother stands, smiling and laughing
and surrounded, as usual, by grinning men. Her popularity went
hand in hand with her beliefs about men: *Men don't like clingy
women. Men don't like aggressive women. Men like amusing, divert-
ing women and lots of emotional support. Men like moderate women
who don't compete with them for the limelight. In other words, men
like women to be fun, to be faithful, to be kind, soft, warm, gentle,
understanding, and to leave them alone.*

My mother, who was a few inches taller than my grandmother,
stands nearby, a beautiful young woman with an intelligent face,
looking frustrated and impatient.

Both women were tall, but unlike me, neither was tall enough
to be considered unfeminine. Instead, their extra few inches of

height seemed to add to their allure. In three generations, our DNA had created a physical stepping stone in the lineage of the women in our family—tall, taller, and too tall. If I wanted to characterize their differences, I would call them the Social Butterfly and the Selfless Homemaker. My grandmother gave her mothering duties to her housekeeper and maid while my mother took those duties to heart.

My grandmother expected the world to revolve around her, and for the most part, it decidedly did, starting with her father, who adored her. She worshipped men and, in the saucy flapper tradition, she rarely wore a pair of underpants. She loved parties; her favourite saying was *You can't fly on one wing*. It meant one drink wasn't enough to have a good time. My mother, on the other hand, was a serious-minded, well-read fifties housewife who didn't drink alcohol and believed mothers should put their family first. She treated most men with suspicion because they made passes at her and tried to spike her Cokes, ignoring her dislike of alcohol. In a moment of confidence, she once told me in all seriousness that the world would be better off without religion, sex, and the male sex.

My mother was an avid reader of novels by Françoise Sagan and Philip Roth. My grandmother's intellectual interests were limited to treacly sayings found in her favourite book, *The Optimist's Good Night* by Florence Hobart Perin.

Although my mother rarely went against my grandmother's wishes, she had surprised her family by marrying my country-doctor father who was eighteen years older and came from a less privileged background. He had been a friend of my grandparents when she met him at a Georgian Bay cottage they rented, and she was already distressing my grandmother with her independent attitude.

He drove up on weekends to visit in his mahogany inboard. Its name, *Thebus*, was printed in gold lettering on its bow. He said he was coming to see her parents. At least that was his story. As for her, she saw him as a refreshing change from her young, irresponsible boyfriends, and the two of them spent their weekends speeding across Georgian Bay in his magnificent boat, her long soft blond hair blowing about her face while he manoeuvred his craft through the choppy waters, avoiding the danger of shoals that lurk just below the surface on this part of the Great Lakes.

He had grown up in the working-class neighbourhood of Cabbagetown, Toronto, but his family had been in the Midland area for generations, so my father knew how to assess the jump-up weather when you were out on the water, and he had no problem either driving through the frequent snowstorms to see patients during the hazardous winters, which started in early November and didn't quit until late April.

Not long ago, at a cottage, I had a vision of the two of them rising like twin genies out of the bay. As I sat relaxing on the hot rocks, their images rose before me un-beckoned. In the vision, she is a tall, pencil-thin blond woman wearing a fashionable 1940s suit and hat while he strolls by her side in his equally dapper pinstripe suit, smoking a cigarette. They look young and carefree, an iconic couple with the promise of a happy life together still ahead of them. She married him during the Second World War, on June 13, 1942, and she wore a full-length blue wedding gown because she considered white bridal dresses a cliché. She forbade wedding speeches for the same reason. I was born on

June 9, 1945, a month and a day after the Germans surrendered to the Allies. My brother, John, was born two years later, on April 15, 1947. On both occasions, my mother had driven herself to the hospital to give birth, stopping by the side of the road to wait out her labour contractions before driving on. My father was too busy with his patients to take her to the hospital.

My mother soon found it lonely being a doctor's wife in a small, isolated town, but there were compensations. It took hours to travel on its gravel roads to Sarnia, and the town must have felt as far away as the Arctic from my grandmother and her demands.

In mid-life, their relationship began to suffer when they both became widows and my grandmother leaned too heavily on my mother for companionship.

My grandmother's situation with her housekeeper Georgette was also deteriorating, even though they used to be friends and Georgette shared my grandmother's love of wrestling. Together they liked to watch the televised matches, which often featured Gorgeous George (George Raymond Wagner), who raised turkeys and owned a cocktail lounge, and Yukon Eric (Eric Holmback), who drove a pink Cadillac and committed suicide by shooting himself in the mouth with a .22-calibre pistol.

My grandmother used to boast that she and Georgette liked "manny men"; that is, men with more muscles than brains. They were also fascinated by the dwarf wrestlers like Little Beaver (Lionel Giroux), who wore a buckskin jacket, and Fuzzy Cupid (Leon Stap), who played the role of Grumpy in a travelling production of Snow White. The truth was that Georgette and my grandmother enjoyed seeing men in all shapes and sizes getting sweaty in skin-tight bikini trunks.

But my grandmother had started taking out her resentment about being old on Georgette, and she claimed she could say anything she liked to her maid. My mother would retort, Mom, you need to be kinder to Georgette. It's not fair.

It likely pleased my grandmother to hear the distress in my mother's voice, because my grandmother didn't want Georgette looking after her. She wanted my mother in Georgette's place. In our close-knit family, older family members were taken care of by widowed or unmarried female relatives, and Aunt Kate was that person when I was growing up. A small, colourless woman, Aunt Kate was a nurse who had no husband or children, and the term *spinster aunt* defined her entirely. At family parties, she was relegated to the sidelines, and the example of her life offered a warning: Don't be a doormat.

THE SAME DAY I saw my mother and my grandmother in the garden, I was back at the lake and reading in the bedroom of my mother's cabin when she appeared at the door, looking frightened. She said Georgette was physically attacking my grandmother.

My mother's brother, my uncle John Cowan, stood behind my mother. The two of them were going into Sarnia to rescue my grandmother. Four hours later they returned and described how they had found my grandmother locked in the first-floor bathroom while Georgette stood outside banging on the door, yelling that she was going to kill my grandmother with her own kitchen knife.

When Georgette saw the pleasant-looking, fair-haired man who was my uncle walking towards her down the hall, she dropped her knife and greeted him in her normal sunny manner, giggling and complimenting him on his appearance in her trilling voice. When he said she needed to stop threatening my grandmother, she ran past him shrieking and waving her arms. My mother and uncle watched in astonishment as Georgette threw open the kitchen door, clutched one of the tall wood verandah pillars with her arms, and burst into wailing sobs.

She wouldn't let go of the pillar, so my mother and uncle called the police. Georgette was still clinging to the verandah pillar screaming and crying when the police officer arrived.

The officer retrieved a white straitjacket from his cruiser and talked to her in a gentle voice until she allowed him to put her arms in the jacket. Then he helped her into his police car.

My mother phoned Georgette's relatives in Brampton and explained the situation and they told her to put Georgette on the train and send her to them. No blood was drawn and neither my mother nor my uncle wanted to press charges. The two of them blamed my grandmother. Of course, having been trained never to contradict my grandmother, they didn't tell her what they thought.

That night, after she put Georgette on the train, my mother told me in a despairing voice that my grandmother would never accept anyone but my mother as a housekeeper. So she and my uncle were going to think of other alternatives. I didn't know what my mother meant, but after my mother's death, I found an entry in her journal from April 25, 1981, which agonized over the pressure she was feeling about putting her mother in a nursing home. Nothing could be worse, in my mother's mind, than dying in such a public place. My grandmother needed not only a housekeeper but a nurse, and my grandmother wanted my mother to be both.

The truth is that I won't sacrifice my life to look after her. I know my course is right but it's very distasteful and makes me feel selfish.

It was touching to hear my mother struggling with whether she should give in to my grandmother's wishes.

As far as my grandmother was concerned, it was my mother's duty to look after her. Unlike many older people, my grandmother had money to hire helpers, but she thought my mother was being selfish not to move in and look after her. I wasn't articulate enough to argue that my mother had a right to live on her own terms. A few years after Georgette tried to attack her, my grandmother fell and was taken to the chronic care ward of the Sarnia hospital. Her health complications required round-the-clock nursing, and she spent four years there before she died in 1986.

I was away on holiday when it happened. I came directly home and my mother had to find suitable mourning clothes for me from her wardrobe. I wasn't shocked by my grandmother's death; I'd known she would die soon, and I used to dread my visits to her in the hospital. The last time I visited, they had put up a bulletin board titled "Reality Check" that listed the day and the month to orient their patients. On this visit, my grandmother thought I was my mother. I tried to tell her who I was but she wouldn't have any of it. So, I sat by her bed, nervously gulping down handfuls of Smarties from the package I had bought for her. Patients weren't allowed to smoke in their rooms, but my grandmother kept asking me to hand her a lighted cigarette and each time I said no, I lowered my eyes. It was upsetting to see how she had devolved into a strange creature whose magnified eyes behind the thick lenses of her eyeglasses regarded me with malevolence. She appeared genderless, a spooky denizen of the hospital ward who had no connection to the woman I knew, the former flapper who loved men and parties and who had told me once that I wouldn't be able to have a writing career when I had a child.

You won't do much writing now, my grandmother said when she found out I was pregnant when I was twenty-eight. We had been drinking tea in her Sarnia duplex, and she had just presented me with a large sandstone statue of a mother holding a nursing baby in her arms. The mother was looking down fondly at the baby slumped against her breast.

I didn't know who had carved the statue or where it came from, and I didn't care. Although I accepted her statue politely, I hid it in my closet and never looked at it again. I had grown out of my childhood notion of not wanting to be a mother. I believed women had the right to balance a career with a home life, and I had all sorts of idealistic notions about what being a parent meant. That it should be easy to live the life of a writer and still be a mother. That being a mother would be part of how I moved in the world, and not my whole life. And why would I want to escape the mother box anyway? I intended to love my child.

In the process of moving house several times I lost the statue my grandmother gave me. Lost accidentally-on-purpose, because her comment had ricocheted through my brain like a bullet from a BB gun hitting a tin target. She might as well have punched me in my pregnant stomach.

I intend to keep writing, I replied. Why wouldn't I?

You won't have time, dear, she replied. You have no idea what's ahead of you.

It was a strange remark coming from someone who had raised

my mother and uncle with a house full of servants. Which is to say my grandmother had plenty of time to do what she wanted when she was a mother. Time to ride horses and lunch with her friends. My grandmother had so much energy my mother used to say that my grandmother should've been the housekeeper, and the housekeeper should have been the lady of the house, because she liked nothing better than to sit and read.

On my last visit, my grandmother had no memory of that afternoon when she told me I would never write again, and she had forgotten all about her happy second marriage to the American man who had loved her when they were young and who married her again fifty years later, after both their partners died. His sons said at his funeral that my grandmother had given their father the ten happiest years of his life. That day in the Sarnia hospital, the central romantic character in what remained of my grandmother's imagination was my mother, Jane, who had refused beyond all reason (in her eyes) to be my grandmother's keeper.

Being a dutiful daughter used to be part of the mother box, the box that no one gets out of no matter how hard we try. It's how all of us come into the world, although as boxes go, it doesn't have much room for the personal needs of the person doing the mothering. A few months before my mother died, I stood over her bed looking down helplessly as she lay trembling from the pain of her ailments. She didn't cry out or complain. She was too stoical. As I stood watching her agony, an image came of a ragged-looking mother bear with twisted claws and bald patches in her fur, and I found myself longing to climb under her still-fearsome paws and shelter there like a bear cub, to hide from the world and let her protect me.

The inferiority-complex box

The personality theory that we now know as the inferiority complex was developed by Alfred Adler, an Austrian psychotherapist who argued that feeling inferior to others plays a key role in human development. When I was growing up, the concept caught on as a meme, and we were all running around saying so-and-so had an inferiority complex or admitting that we had an inferiority complex ourselves, which is why we did what we did. Today the word *trauma* is used in much the same way to explain human behaviour. Femmie Smith's trauma was her size, although she wouldn't have used that word to describe her unhappiness then. She used to be six foot one, until she asked a surgeon to cut four inches out of her femur bones so she could be the more feminine height of five foot ten.

So, it was obvious to me when I was sent off as a young journalist to interview Femmie that she was suffering from an inferiority complex.

On slow days at the tabloid newspaper where I worked as an education reporter, the city desk would give me what they called "colour" stories. Once I swam in a bikini allegedly to investigate pollution in the Toronto Harbour. They ran my story on the front page with a mock-serious photo of me diving into the lake and a caption: *To Swim or Not to Swim in our Murky Harbour. The Telegram's reporter Susan Swan kicked up her heels and dove into the dark waters of Toronto bay for a look. She found it so murky, she couldn't see very well . . .*

I'm really doing a headstand on a sand bar, and the photo shows my legs sticking out of the water, legs that hadn't been shortened like the vulnerable thighbones of Femmie Smith.

And now I was facing the woman who had undergone surgery because her height had caused her too much anguish. Femmie had spent eight months in Toronto's Orthopaedic and Arthritic Hospital after two operations, one on each thighbone, with two months in a cast for each leg.

When she answered her door and saw me standing there, her mouth fell open. You could have the operation too! she exclaimed.

I smiled politely and nodded although I had never entertained the notion of shortening my height, even after my first husband had thoughtlessly suggested it when we were teenagers. I was twenty-two and busy getting ahead with my writing. She was the one (not me) who had an inferiority complex. I was done (or so I told myself) with my terror about being unfeminine. The photograph taken that day shows me towering over Femmie, looking at her skeptically while I hold my notepad. I had on my sixties costume: a blond fall (I was too busy reporting to wash my hair), a very short miniskirt, and a see-through blouse. *If people are going to stare you might as well give them something to stare at.* I sometimes wore stacked gladiator sandals as part of my defiance, but that day I had on flats.

Femmie was standing in the doorway of her modest suburban home in Newmarket, Ontario, and I could see that although she had once been my height, she was now several inches shorter than me, and she was pretty, with cropped, curly dark hair and a round friendly face. There were no signs of her operation except that her arms looked too long for her torso.

She led me into her living room, offering to introduce me to the orthopaedic surgeon who could cut inches off my thighbones, which, she claimed, would bring me the relief she felt. When her mother brought in a plate of sandwiches, Femmie pressed me again to talk to her surgeon and, once more, I demurred. It was a relief when she began telling me why she had her operation. Her mother was five foot ten and a half and her father was six-two (my height), but of course I didn't mention that. I sat there, stunned, my notepad on my lap, scribbling down what she said, trying to radiate sympathy while feeling secretly horrified by what she had done.

This is what I was finding out:

She and her parents were Dutch immigrants and most of Femmie's suffering over her height happened in the Netherlands when she was a young teenager. She quit junior high and did her schoolwork at home in order to avoid being mocked by her schoolmates. She stopped going out in public because she hated people making wisecracks about her size, and she did all her shopping by telephone. She didn't attend parties. She was bitter about the time a boy had asked her to dance and then ran away as soon as she stood up. As a teenager, she insisted on sleeping in a crib with her head and feet pressed up to the headboard and end of the bed in the hopes that this arrangement would stop her from growing. It was a literal manifestation of my own childhood prayer for my head to stop its march to the ceiling.

It was strange that the Dutch children had been so cruel, because the Dutch are the world's tallest people. According to Rachel Pannett in a 2021 article in the *Washington Post*, "The World's Tallest Population Is Shrinking." Their height started increasing in the 1950s, thanks in part to the Dutch milk program in the schools; only recently has it begun to slightly decline. So, it wasn't as if Femmie had been six foot one in a Mediterranean culture where people tend to be shorter.

Over the past thirty years, anthropometric historians have done studies that show height is a biological shorthand that measures a society's well-being. According to *New Yorker* staff writer Burkhard Bilger in his essay "The Height Gap," published March 28, 2004, height variations within a population are largely genetic, but height variations between populations are mostly environmental and nutrition has a lot to do with it.

Height spurts occur in infancy, from the years six to eight, and during adolescence. Bilger says one of the reasons the Dutch are so tall may be because they have the best infant care in the world.

Northern European populations have grown taller than American populations, according to Bilger. Immigration to America may be partly responsible for that lack of growth, because many immigrants are shorter than Americans when they arrive. But it's also related to nutrition and the American love of fast foods.

During the First World War, Bilger says, the average American man was two inches taller than the average German. Since 1955, Northern Europeans on average are three inches taller than the average American. In 2004, when Bilger wrote his essay, the average American man was only five foot nine and a half, less than an inch taller than the average height of soldiers during the Revolutionary War.

Bilger notes that the National Center for Health Statistics, which conducts periodic surveys of as many as thirty-five thousand Americans, says women born in the late 1950s and early 1960s had an average height of just under five foot five. Those born a decade later are one-third of an inch shorter. According to the Greatlist website, the average height of both Canadian and

American women is currently five foot four, while the average height of Canadian men is five foot ten and one inch.

During Femmie's operation, Dr. James E. Bateman cut out a four-inch section of her femur, the large bone that runs from the knee to the hip joint. The ends of her femurs were brought together and fastened with a metal plate designed for her at the Orthopaedic and Arthritic Hospital. Then the bone that had been removed was grafted onto the femur to give it extra strength. Muscles, blood vessels, and nerves were left untouched because they would shorten on their own. Each operation took three hours, and Femmie endured endless months of physiotherapy sessions afterwards to make her thigh muscles strong again.

This was an unusual surgery because Femmie's surgeon didn't do height reduction operations unless there was a good medical reason, like one leg being shorter than the other. But Dr. Bateman said he had reduced Femmie's height because she had "severe psychological trauma" over her size, and not because she wanted to be shorter than her boyfriend. In a Canadian newspaper story dated September 22, 1967, Dr. Bateman is quoted as saying that Femmie had a definite physical abnormality. It's hard to imagine a medical doctor saying now that a young woman who stood six foot one in her stocking feet was physically abnormal.

Fashions change. Now short men and women seek out the painful ordeal of leg-altering surgery. Short women who do it sometimes complain that they're treated like children at work, while short men say they need to be taller in order to get respect and avoid insults like *garden gnome*.

An early limb-lengthening technique, known as the Modular Rail System, used a surgical nail attached to an external frame that fits around the leg. More advanced techniques are now used, and these surgeries encourage bone growth, which adds inches to the length of the leg. Although leg-lengthening still involves an uncomfortable operation and a year of physical therapy, patients who want to have a leg shortened have an easier time now. If Femmie had been able to have modern orthopaedic surgery, she would have been able to walk out of the hospital the day of her surgery.

I COULDN'T FIND any records of Dr. Bateman doing another height reduction surgery like the one he did for Femmie. Nor was I able to find any information about what happened to Femmie, who may be dead or living under a married name. If she is still alive, I imagine our conversation might go something like this:

Me: I used to think you had an inferiority complex. It didn't occur to me that I had one too. Do you have any regrets about your surgery?

Femmie: No regrets. But I'm sorry I suggested you should get your legs shortened.

Me: Well, there are so many ways to make yourself smaller. You know what I mean? Limiting your options, not reaching out for what you want and going along with what others expect of you. When you and I met, I thought it was ludicrous to shorten your legs, but I was making myself smaller by doing the traditional things that young people my age were expected to do then: I was engaged to be married and working at a nine-to-five job at a newspaper when I wanted to write novels. Don't think, write, a city desk editor advised me. Excellent advice to a journalist on a breaking news story. Not for a young novelist like myself about to marry someone who didn't understand my writerly ambitions. The eventual unhappiness that resulted from my decision meant I had to torch the box I had placed myself in, an act that required an enormous emotional and physical effort that would reverberate through my life and the life of my young daughter for years to come.

The tradition box

As soon as I interviewed the university professor in his office, I knew he would be a perfect husband for my mother. Let's call him the Prospect. I wanted him to take my mother off my hands so I could get on with my life. And now here he is knocking at the door of my mother's comfortable Forest Hill home in Toronto, which she had purchased not long after my father's death. The Prospect is looking his part in the classic dress of a 1960s egghead, a tweed jacket with leather patches on its elbows, his pipe tilted sideways out of his mouth, his smooth gray hair trimmed neatly back from his high forehead and not flopping into his eyes or dripping in long unwashed strands onto his shoulders, like some of the hippie boys I knew.

I imagine him as more outline than man, more symbol than person, because in my early twenties I'm not good yet at seeing men as full human beings. And despite growing up with a brother, I've spent too many years in a boarding school where men were the exotic other, privileged boys from wealthy families who mailed us letters scribbled in longhand, billets-doux stuffed into envelopes stamped with the crest of their private school.

Men haven't quite attained the status of real people, and it will be a few years before that happens. So perhaps this is why I so easily assume, without thinking of her needs, that this man is perfect for my mother. I have already added up the pros on my list and ignored the cons.

1. He's an English professor at a prominent Toronto university and he likes to talk about novels. (So does she.)
2. He's her age, forty-four.
3. He's also attractive, and she's beautiful.
   What more can you ask?

That evening, my mother, our hostess and resident domestic goddess, stands behind me, her golden hair perfectly coiffed after a perm at her hairdresser. She wears a tweed skirt and a pale blue blouse with a string of pearls. She's big on pastels, and she used to make me wear light colours as a child even though pastels were the signature trademark of her taste, not mine. The blue of her eyes matches her blouse, the soft blond shade of her hair—the overall effect is all of a piece.

I have no idea what she's thinking. She's far too polite to show it, although I doubt if she has guessed what I'm scheming to do. Or perhaps she has already figured it out and she is cooking our dinner to humour me, and now the smell of the chicken roasting in the oven is drifting slowly through the house in delectable gusts. I bought a bottle of Mateus, the sickeningly sweet Portu-

guese rosé my college friends and I think is the height of sophisti-
cation. It's going to be a feast. She has even baked one of her fluffy
angel cakes for dessert.

If she knows I'm trying to matchmake that evening, she gives
no sign, and her formal manners stop me (and likely him) from
sensing her thoughts. He doesn't know what I'm up to either
because I've asked him on the pretext that I would like to get to
know him better in order to do a good write-up on him for the
newspaper, and I expect him to have the same gushing reaction as
the boys I've brought home from university. Your mother! What a
knockout! one of them exclaimed after eating a dish of my mother's
celebrated scrambled eggs (cook very slowly with heaps of butter
and no milk) along with marmalade toast.

In 1967, when the Prospect came for dinner, I was living
with my mother after graduating from McGill. It was the year of
the Summer of Love, when over one hundred thousand young
people, most of them hippies, had gathered in the neighbourhood of Haight-Ashbury in San Francisco. Inspired by the Beat
Generation of the fifties, they were protesting the Vietnam War
and consumerism, values I shared, although their communes
where women played subservient domestic roles filled me with
dread.

That year, I was working long hours like my father, covering
campus marches and demonstrations for my daily newspaper. It
published five daily editions, so reporters needed to keep updat-
ing their breaking news stories. When I wasn't exhausted from
reporting, I staggered up to a room in the attic of my mother's
house and tried to write fiction on my Remington Electric. I
usually gave up after typing a few sentences, or I started rewriting

the short stories I'd written at college. I was spinning my wheels and I knew it, but I didn't understand that writing fiction required long uninterrupted blocks of time that let you daydream your way into a novel or short story.

IN AN ATTEMPT to put our family back together following the upheaval after my father's death, my mother had moved with my brother and me to Toronto. She expected me to go to university there, and, instead, the next fall, I had insisted on going to McGill. As I was boarding the train for Montreal, my mother collapsed weeping into my arms. She said she couldn't bear to see me go, and I told her I'd come back and live with her after my graduation. I felt about that promise much the way the fairytale heroine felt about offering Rumpelstiltskin her first-born. I'll come back, I shouted from the steps of the coach. I'll come back and live with you and things will be all right again.

It was what I needed to tell myself in order to go. I was rushing towards freedom with a smile on my face, deliberately ignoring my mother's expectation that a good daughter stays home with her widowed mother. She hadn't wanted to be my grandmother's live-in companion after her stepfather died, but she seemed to expect me to be hers at a time when I was trying to get on with my own life. My grandmother, who was still alive, thought I should stay home with my mother too. Even today, I never enter Montreal without being overwhelmed by excitement, the old heady feeling that I'm getting away with something. I loved my undergraduate courses in English and philosophy, and the reporting I did for the college newspaper, the *McGill Daily*. I especially enjoyed my writing workshop with the late Hugh MacLennan, the most famous Canadian writer of his generation. He prided himself on being a student of physiognomy and he allowed me in because he said my clear eyes and delicately shaped chin told him I had common sense. In his workshop, he claimed that the big earlobes of a politician like the American president Lyndon Johnson were proof of Johnson's empathetic nature. MacLennan had large earlobes himself, and a great deal of sympathy for young writers, even if he tended to be extra hard on the men in our class.

WHILE I'M WORKING at the Toronto newspaper, my mother runs the house and cooks my meals just as she did for my father. We're following the traditional pattern of the intense mother-daughter relationships in my family. When the men went missing for one reason or another, the women relied on each other for understanding and companionship. In those years, that's where true familial intimacy could be found, at least as far as intimacy was understood, but I was finding my mother's emotional dependence on me exhausting. She said she couldn't share her difficulties with anyone else because her friends were older cronies of my dead father and they didn't understand her problems. She felt trapped in the wrong social milieu but she scoffed at my suggestion that she get a job so she could meet new people. The longer I stayed with her the more our lives were becoming entwined, and the two of us talked about renting a house in Edinburgh while I worked on the city's daily newspaper. I wasn't sure spending a year away with my mother was the right thing for me to do, but I felt I owed her.

She was a stay-at-home mother and my first mentor and

champion. She had wanted to be a writer herself and decided she lacked literary talent, so she enthusiastically encouraged my writing after she caught me memorizing the bedtime stories she read to my brother and me (stories like *The Tale of Peter Rabbit* by Beatrix Potter). I had memorized the stories in those books to impress her, and she was thrilled. When I was an adult, she told me she'd made sure I was never denied any book I was interested in. Soon I was doing what she hoped I would do—I was writing stories myself. There were plenty of subjects to write about, although the most obvious subject took a while to present itself—my body.

In grade seven, I wrote a precocious short story about a man in a humdrum marriage titled "The Life of Henry B. Small." When my teacher accused me of plagiarism, claiming no eleven-year-old could create a story that sophisticated, my mother rushed to my defence and he backed down.

My teacher couldn't have known that by the time I was ten, my school friends came to my house on Saturdays to hear my stories.

One of my stories involved Frank Carl, a real-life coarse, pudgy man who ran a riding stable outside town. He flirted with us, and I wrote stories about him trapping one of my friends in his barn, exploratory tales of sexual initiation that made us burst into horrified giggles. The Frank Carl stories were influenced by the copy of the novel *Peyton Place* hidden under a layer of cotton batten in my mother's jewellery drawer. An instant bestseller when it came out in 1956, it exposed the hypocrisy of small-town life in America and explicitly described sex between men and women. It was a thrilling revelation to discover that female characters could be as interested in sex as the men.

Not all the controversial books were hidden in my mother's

jewellery drawer. The Book of the Month Club sent her a cross-section of sophisticated adult novels. Books like *The Quiet American* by Graham Greene, even *Lolita* by Vladimir Nabokov. At the age of twelve, I read everything I could get my hands on, Canadian novels like *Swamp Angel* by Ethel Wilson and *A Girl of the Limberlost* by American naturalist Gene Stratton-Porter along with British classics like *Jane Eyre* by Charlotte Brontë and *Wuthering Heights* by her sister Emily. I also read countless books about science and psychology.

But writers can be prickly and outspoken, and my mother didn't realize what having one in the family meant. She saw the future me as a latter-day Virginia Woolf, looking saintly and pensive in her Edwardian photographs, although I wasn't anything like Virginia Woolf and Virginia Woolf wasn't as serene as that image of her suggested either.

And that's where the forty-something English professor comes in. I'd met the Prospect on a journalism assignment for *The Telegram*. Its managing editor wanted me to do a series called "The New Academics" because he was certain more iconoclasts like Marshall McLuhan were hiding in the academic study halls, and he told me to discover who they were and write about them. I never came across anyone remotely like McLuhan but I did manage to find the Prospect, whose specialty was a popular undergraduate course on the progress of romantic love through the ages, and that leads me back to the fateful dinner.

There is a large living room and a den in my mother's home as well as a recreation room overlooking a back garden that descends in several levels to a lane only a few feet from the ravine where burglars were said to lurk at night in order to break into the nearby homes. The main living room, carpeted in a robin's-egg blue, has windows on both sides of the long rectangular room and a pretty fireplace whose hearth is decorated in painted tiles. It's a welcoming room, and my mother often sits in it, looking like the perfect chatelaine who will jump up and offer you food and drink the moment you walk in the door.

In my hospitable family, the comfort of a guest is of utmost importance, and it's offered to the Prospect the night he arrives at our house. I'm waiting for him to ogle my mother as we sit chatting, but the Prospect keeps directing questions to me about the life of a reporter. He says working on a tabloid is an inferior job for someone like me who graduated with an English degree from one of Canada's finest universities, and he presses me for reasons why I'm there. I consider complaining about the slow days for campus news, when editors send me out to conduct gritty interviews with families who have just lost a member in a horrific murder or construction accident. Then there are the unwanted midnight phone calls after another paper publishes a scoop on a campus protest that I failed to report, and how in the dawn light I needed to leave for the office to paste together a matching story cribbed from their front-page article.

Instead, as we sit talking with my mother, I deflect his questions back to her. Tell him, I say, about the books you're reading, and she obliges by trotting out a suitable answer. His face brightens when she confides that she is enjoying the new collection of stories by Alice Munro, *Dance of the Happy Shades*, but when she starts in on the vulgarity of Mordecai Richler's new novel *Cocksure*, his expression darkens. It's as if he's pulled down a blind, and to keep the conversation moving, I bring up Virginia Woolf's essay "Mr. Bennett and Mrs. Brown," in which Woolf spoke about the need for writers of her generation to use new literary devices like disjointed narratives in order to convey the state of modern life.

I point out that Richler's ribald language is meant to reflect the frank way our society talks about sex. Now it's my mother's turn to shut down. I stop in mid-sentence. She throws me a disapproving glance and hurries off to the kitchen to get coffee. As soon as she's gone, I ask in a whisper if he likes my mother.

It's you I'm interested in, he replies, catching me off guard. He says he thought I asked him home to get my mother's approval. This isn't how my plan was supposed to work, and for a moment, I don't know what to say. We sit looking at each other, expressions of frustration on both our faces. I'm so sorry, I finally blurt, I have a boyfriend.

You might have told me that, he says, sounding miffed. He gets up and leaves without thanking my mother, who is in the kitchen making the coffee. When she comes back into the living room, carrying the coffee tray, she looks in surprise at his empty chair and then her face relaxes.

He's a little old for you, she says as she pours me a coffee. But he's a nice man. Is he your latest beau?

I shake my head, feeling like a fool. My matchmaking is a failure, like so many failures of understanding between my mother and myself. My attempt to hand over my responsibility for her well-being to a potential stepfather has collapsed. Even worse, I've been as insensitive as my eighty-something grandmother, who also wants to marry her off. And just as she has done with her own mother, my mother is determined to resist my efforts to make her do things she has no interest in doing. But as it turns out, it will be me, and not my mother, who is the next woman in our family to step into the marriage box.

The marriage box

1.

A few years before I moved back in with my mother, I brought Lionel, the college boy whose fraternity pin I wore, home to meet her. Here's another scene from the memory bank:

Lionel and I are chatting on the landing of my mother's house in Toronto when a green sports car pulls into our driveway and a young man in a three-piece suit steps out.

It's Barry, a Toronto boy I dated as a teenager. His family came up to a Georgian Bay cottage near ours, and he was the boyfriend who jokingly suggested I cut several inches off my thighs so I wouldn't turn into a giantess like Anna Swan. He is working now as a stockbroker. He lives near my mother and often drops in on her for a visit.

Do you see the determined look on his face? Lionel says, pointing down at Barry. That man is after you!

I burst out laughing. I considered Barry old-fashioned. The fact that he is wearing a bespoke three-piece sets him apart from the other young men of the sixties, especially someone like Lionel, who has on dirty jeans and a shirt with a Mao collar.

At that moment, Barry looks up and waves, and we come down. Barry says hello to me and nods dismissively at Lionel. Later, Barry tells me he didn't like the look of Lionel. He had a point. Lionel was troubled, a young man with too many problems for me, and a few months later, when I broke up with him, Lionel threatened to kill me.

The almost-murder happened like this:

Lionel asked me for lunch in his Montreal rooming house along with our mutual friend, Bill, and I accepted because I felt guilty about the breakup. That day, he wouldn't look me in the eye. Mumbling in a weird, strained voice, Lionel ushered me upstairs and into his bedsit where incense was burning in small brass bowls on the kitchen table. He admired Arabic cultures, and blankets with Moroccan designs billowed slightly from their place on the walls. The atmosphere in the room felt deeply creepy, like the setting for a diabolical ritual whose meaning was known only to him—the cloying smell of incense; the wall hanging with tapestries the colour of ancient stains of menstrual blood; and lastly, Lionel himself looking menacing in a bulky Moroccan caftan that he'd purchased on vacation.

A pair of shrivelled pork chops sizzled in an electric frying pan on the kitchen table. The meat bristled with fat and I guessed he had bought the cheapest food he could find. It was a point of leftist honour for him to serve what he thought poor French-Canadian families ate for dinner. Only two places had been set next to the frying pan.

I looked around his bedsit. Where's Bill? I asked.

Bill couldn't make it, Lionel replied.

I felt a prickle of anxiety. Only a week before, Lionel had stood in the shadows of my Montreal apartment building waiting for me. I'd been at the greasy spoon around the corner, and as I started towards the steps of my building, a caped figure rushed out of the darkness. Flapping his long arms, he cried: The owl of Minerva spreads its wings only with the falling of the dusk! He was quoting the nineteenth-century German philosopher Georg Wilhelm Friedrich Hegel, who believed philosophers don't understand a historical era until it's over. His words that night had a sinister meaning: Only now, since you broke up with me, do I understand the perfidy of your love.

What a fool I'd been! As I turned to leave his bedsit, he grabbed something long and silvery from a nearby closet. There was a flash of metal as he charged towards me, raising his sword and thrusting the tip at my heart. Prepare to die, he cried. Because I'm going to kill you.

Let's freeze this horrifying moment with his sword pointing at my chest while I point out my reaction, because I had no way of knowing if he was going to carry out his threat. He said he intended to kill me, and the ferocious look on his face felt real. He was taller than me, and his muscled body was quivering with menace, so I had to take him at his word. I was shocked and surprised and then felt a surge of volcanic anger. How dare he invite me to lunch on false pretenses and tell me he was going to kill me!

My anger came from being discounted in demoralizing ways. The adults who said: Don't forget, you're just a girl. Or, if I sounded confident: You think well of yourself for a girl. Or from experiences like winning the Junior Midland golf championship when the boy received a huge silver cup while girls like me went empty-handed because we weren't considered worthy of a trophy. And so on.

In those days, young women like me expected men to do

awful things, although I didn't experience the same ongoing harassment as my large-breasted roommate who had to deal with obscene phone callers, or men who uttered bestial guttural sounds in their throats when they noticed her chest. And as a white woman, I don't experience the harsh realities of racism. However, the drip-drip effect of misogyny is cumulative, and in situations where men try to take advantage, rage can shoot through me and I fight back before I realize what I'm doing. My body was too big to fit the gender script of the times, but being big is an advantage in fights like the brawl that happened at McGill when a friend's much taller older brother attacked me. I was making him coffee to thank him for driving me home from a party when he announced that he was going to teach me how to treat a man. My first mistake, according to him, had been refusing to let him light my cigarettes. I wasn't sure if he meant he was going to try to rape me or beat me up, or both. Without waiting for my response, he grabbed my wrist and threw me against the living room wall of my apartment. I immediately threw him back against the opposite wall and soon we were grunting and panting from physical exertion, the way drunks groan and sigh in a bar fight. He was stronger, and he exuded a terrifying ferocity. Luckily for me, just as my strength started to slip away, my roommate came home and asked what was going on. He rushed past her and fled down the stairs.

My instinct to fight back started in public school when I used to watch *Dragnet*, a popular crime show on television. Its star Jack Webb would order the criminal to give up his weapon. You don't really want to kill me, bud, Jack Webb would say. The criminal would shrug and hand over his gun. That's how it was done in the cop shows of the 1950s. Even criminals had a conscience (or at least a heart) and could respond to fair treatment.

So that afternoon with Lionel, I thought of Jack Webb and told Lionel in my sternest voice: You don't really want to do this. I was standing at my full height, like the actor in a Greek tragedy who summons up all their moral courage and physical resolve in order to meet their fate. Everyone has these moments when they are fully inside their bodies and experiencing their personal authority.

Lionel didn't move, and he kept his sword pointing at my breast.

You heard me, I yelled. Give me that! Without thinking what I was doing, I grabbed the blade.

The sword clattered to the floor. You were always too strong for me, he said in a voice so low I could barely hear him.

I glanced down at my hand, expecting to see blood, but there wasn't any. He was using his duelling sword, whose edges were blunt. However, he had removed the rubber guard on its sharp tip. It can still give you a small wound or poke out your eye.

I was going to kill Bill too, he mumbled. I know you're sleeping with him.

Bill wasn't my lover. Turning my back on Lionel, I rushed out of his bedsit.

When I told Bill about it later, he said: It was kind of cute, you know, romantic even. According to Bill, killing me was obviously doomed, and he pointed out that duelling swords were bendy and relatively harmless. Who murders anybody with a weapon like that? Bill asked. More likely, Bill said, my ex was staging a dramatic protest in the hopes of me taking him back.

I told Bill Lionel's behaviour wasn't cute. I didn't realize he was threatening me with a duelling sword until I grabbed the blade and felt its blunt edges. I was trying to save my life. However, Lionel offered the same rationale as Bill when he called me up years later to ask my advice about his daughter becoming a writer. He described the incident as campus hi-jinks, although I experienced genuine terror that day in his boarding house bedsit.

IN THE SPRING of that year, I started seeing Lionel again.

I didn't tell anyone. I was doing it to get him to stop harassing me and I felt ashamed of myself. Years later, I read about compliance as a strategy that some women use to deal with assault, and it makes sense. Sometimes it can feel like the safest thing to do is to give in and wait for the unpleasantness to pass.

That spring at McGill, the author Constance Beresford-Howe, who also taught a college workshop in creative writing, said I could write a novel for my MA thesis. I refused her exciting offer. That decision set back by a decade my ambition to write fiction, but returning to McGill for graduate work would have meant dealing with Lionel.

If I had done the MA, chances are I wouldn't have gone back to live with my mother after college and I wouldn't have married the first boy I dated, when I was fourteen. I would have started my career as a novelist instead of a reporter. Maybe I would have become known as a novelist earlier. But the years of working as a professional journalist gave me skills I use to this day. Perhaps nothing is ever really lost. What appears to be gone forever can emerge in a new, unexpected form.

The most remarkable thing about the college boys trying to assault me was that I didn't find these experiences remarkable. Instead, I put what happened behind me and moved on. In those years, women my age were expected to stickhandle assaults the way we managed snowstorms and traffic jams. We were told it was up to us to set the tone so men didn't take advantage of us. This advice gave me a sense of agency, but it was woefully misleading. It wasn't all up to me. And it was too much to expect that it should be.

As soon as I graduated and moved back to Toronto, I stopped seeing Lionel. And for the first time, I started meeting men who had organized their lives more responsibly than mixed-up college boys.

2.

Barry was four years older than me and he had already worked for eight years as a broker. I was very fond of him because he was unpretentious and dependable and confident. The year I came home to live with my mother, he proposed marriage, and when I refused, he said it usually took women two years of working at a job before they were ready to marry and he was prepared to wait. I laughed at his old-fashioned notion that women would prefer the chores of a housewife to a job like mine. But when he kept his word and proposed again two years later, I accepted. This time he offered to support me so I could write fiction, and I thought he understood my determination to become a novelist. His steadiness felt reassuring at a time when I was besieged by men asking me out. All sorts of men I didn't know, men who might upset my plan to write or be physically dangerous if I didn't do what they wanted.

When she heard what I had done, my mother predicted that I would grow bored with him. The know-it-all tone in her voice felt irritating, and, partly to defy her, I went ahead with the engagement. For years afterwards, I would ask myself why I decided to get married when what I was really interested in was writing fiction. I wasn't pregnant. My work as a journalist was building my confidence, and the future looked full of promise. But instead of moving ahead with what I wanted to do, I was charging into a situation about which I had strong misgivings. Unlike me, my husband-to-be had traditional values. Was the experience of the violent college boys too alarming? Or did I get married because I thought I needed a man by my side to make my life plan work?

There was also my height, although my sudden, unexpected popularity meant I could no longer see myself as a rejected, ungainly wallflower. The feeling of being oversized lingered, as it does for many of us who have bodies that don't fit the norm. A fear like mine may seem overstated and even absurd, but a poor physical self-image often feels more real than the face we see in the mirror. This is how my thinking went, although I wouldn't have been able to say it in words at the time: I must be attractive—sort of; a number of people say so. But my appearance feels like a dress that doesn't belong to me.

Of course, the way my size was shaping my reactions was as invisible to me as the rivers that run underground beneath cities, an unseen current pushing me towards choices that weren't always in my best interest. It was the silent engine that drove me forward the same way it led Femmie Smith to make a harsh physical bargain that let her take up less space in the world.

I MARRIED MY husband at the editorial boardroom of our newspaper when I was twenty-four. A Jewish rabbi who worked for *The Telegram* performed the ceremony. A few months later, I quit my newspaper job to write fiction, and we moved into a spacious apartment in the upscale Toronto neighbourhood of Rosedale with two bedrooms and a study for me. It was the perfect writer's den for someone like myself. But just as I began working on my first book, Barry bought a Victorian mansion across the street without telling me and said we had to start packing to move into our new home, a house so capacious that walking into each room was like entering a new country. The house was built in the Romanesque Revival style with five floors and six bedrooms, not including the summer sleeping quarters overlooking a ravine.

After we moved in, my novel went nowhere. Our new home was rarely quiet. My husband thought nothing of rearranging the furniture while I was trying to write, and friends often dropped by to play the pinball machine he had installed in the front hall. Then, once again without telling me, he sold the mansion after we had lived there for a few months and bought a semi-detached bay-and-gable townhouse near the Yorkville coffee house where I'd once had a summer job as a waitress. We moved a second time. He had either forgotten his promise to pay our expenses so I could write fiction, or he didn't take it seriously in the first place. After we married, he insisted that I pay for my personal needs, so I wrote magazine articles right up to the day my daughter was born because I was too proud to ask him for money.

My novel was soon in the toilet. Meanwhile, a crowd of wealthy, fun-loving friends had swept us up in their lifestyle, and I squandered the time I needed to write fiction on roving with them from one high-end restaurant to another, looking for the perfect menu.

An unpublished poem I wrote sums up that period in my life:

The woman you see before you
drinks too much
and talks too loudly,
guilty that she is more
than she appears.

A friend who knew me well said I looked as if I was posing as a rich young Toronto matron, but my long, fair hair was too wild and my dress was hiked up at the wrong angles, and nothing rang true about my performance.

I was sitting with friends at an expensive restaurant one evening when a journalist pal stopped by my table. What are you doing with those people? He nodded at my husband and the others who were on their second round of liqueurs, talking volubly with each other. Nearby, some television producers I knew were buying drinks for their young mistresses while brightly coloured ceiling flags fluttered in currents from the air conditioner. The atmosphere felt deflated. The listless mood was typical of Toronto at the start of the 1970s, as if the city was taking a breath after the wild trailblazing party of the sixties.

His question unsettled me. He saw my situation. I was the wrong partygoer in the wrong place at the wrong time, living in a way that had nothing to do with my aspirations. What on earth had I been thinking? And why fritter away my time with partygoers when I wanted to write novels? Not long afterwards, I was shocked to learn I was going to have a baby even though I had taken precautions.

I have a highly developed inner critic whose admonishments are likely connected to my mother and her perfectionism, the strategy she used to ward off the scrutiny we get as women. *Just look at the mess you've made,* my inner critic shrieked. *How on earth could you go and do something so dumb? Don't you have even a shred of common sense?*

As it happens, giving birth to my daughter, Samantha, turned out to be one of the luckiest things that I have ever experienced. It gave me a small person to love and forced me to grow up and stop pretending I had years to create the life I wanted. Before I found out I was pregnant with my daughter, time had been a secret in my bones.

It took me a while to figure out what to do. An abortion felt unthinkable. The baby was a girl and she was due on my birthday. Surely there was a way to make my marriage work. After all, I'd navigated difficult relationships at boarding school. Why couldn't I figure out how to live with my husband and our child and still do the writing I wanted?

I started throwing the I Ching three or four times a day, questioning the oracle about my troubles and how I could resolve my situation. Oracle abuse, some call it. The first time I tossed the pennies, up popped the first hexagram, the Creative. Other times, it was hexagram 56, the Wanderer. It didn't matter how often I threw the coins, the hexagrams felt too ambiguous for someone like myself, searching frantically for a *yes* or *no* answer.

I was the one who had chosen marriage to a conservative businessman. And now I was about to bring a child into a relationship that wasn't working. I had to find a solution.

When our attempt to work out our problems with a counsellor failed, I started seeing a psychotherapist on my own. In one session, I raised my question about combining writing with raising a family, expecting a friendly lecture about working harder on my marriage. Instead, the therapist's face grew solemn. I'm overreacting, aren't I? I persisted. Surely I don't have to hurt my husband and baby daughter by upending our lives. He shook his head sadly. You have very real concerns about where your life is headed, he replied. If you don't address your concerns, you will find yourself living in a situation that doesn't give you the fulfillment you seek, and there's a possibility you'll wake up one day and wonder what happened to your ambition to be a writer. I sat stunned. It wasn't the reassurance I craved. He was saying my concerns needed to be taken seriously, and the rest was up to me.

His advice brought up the scary possibility of living as a single mother. But the future was becoming clear: if I wanted to fulfill myself, I needed to change my life.

My ex-husband and I have become good friends, and these pages aren't the right place to relitigate the story of my divorce, which is a story about the familiar plight of two young people who marry early only to discover their partner isn't the right person for their needs. Yet something has to be said and this is a simple way of saying it: I married a man who seemed to be waiting for me to turn into my traditional mother (something that was never going to happen), and my goal was to write novels. So I left the comfortable upper-class life I might have had with him to live a life of my own making—poor or prosperous, I didn't know. I made an instinctive choice, and instinctive choices are sometimes the right ones. They aren't necessarily wrong because they're instinctive.

So, not long after my counselling session, I told my husband I wanted a divorce and he reluctantly agreed. On one of our last nights out together, he and I went to see the movie *Paper Moon* with the real-life father-and-daughter pair of actors Ryan and Tatum O'Neal. The movie celebrated the bond between a con artist and his child and it made us both weep. Afterwards, I reassured him that he would never lose his daughter, and we decided on joint custody as a way to handle caring for our child. Now there was nothing for it but to climb out of the marriage box with my young daughter and get on with the life I wanted.

Part Two

THE ART OF
BEING FAME-ISH

IN 1974, I pack up my eight-month-old baby, Samantha, and drive over to a seedy downtown co-op to start my new life.

My mother always said I wanted to be poor, and the co-op is suitably rundown. The floor of the hall is covered with a faded red runner that looks like it hasn't been cleaned in years. The tattered runner also carpets the tall staircase that leads to the shabby upstairs of what was once the sleeping quarters of a well-to-do Toronto family.

The front hallway is long and gloomy with dirty stucco walls, and there is a grubby kitchen on the first floor where the young dancers and musicians stake out their territories in separate cupboards marked with their names. The setting feels make-do verging on derelict.

There are also two bedrooms, a bathroom, and a large living room with a brick fireplace on the first floor. Six more bedrooms are on the second and third floors. Two of those are mine and they are at the front of the house. There's a working fireplace beside my bed; my two rooms must have once been the master bedroom.

There is only one bathroom for second- and third-floor tenants like myself, a steamy, fetid room with a stained shower curtain and posh, out-of-place red broadloom that retains the moisture from countless showers. Every bedroom in the house is filled.

It's exactly the kind of home my mother disdains. As indeed she does the first time she enters the house, glancing quickly and disapprovingly at the sink full of dirty dishes in the kitchen.

Despite my mother's disapproval, I chose the co-op because it was cheap and near my daughter's daycare. My ex and I had joint custody, so I didn't ask for financial support from him until eight years later, when our divorce agreement was amended to give me a modest annual stipend. The rent at the co-op was $200 a month for a bedroom and the adjoining room for Samantha, my baby girl, who would rotate every two weeks between our homes. I intended to live humbly in order to de-privilege myself, and like many romantic attempts at virtue, my plan had its faux underbelly. Even though I was on my own, making money and paying my own way, trying to get rid of privilege, as Gloria Steinem said once, is like throwing away a boomerang. I knew my family would lend me money if I ran into trouble.

To pay my bills, I planned to do an assortment of freelance jobs while I wrote fiction, and for only a few hundred dollars a month I had the run of an enormous Edwardian house that served my needs relatively well.

The co-op offered more space, both physically and metaphorically, for me to become who I wanted to be, and it had the added benefit of looking completely unlike the comfortable, well-kept houses of my childhood.

My mother likely felt a mix of emotions seeing my new quarters: frustration, despair, and possibly guilt that she'd failed to instill in me her love of beauty and fine things.

She was too familiar with my stubbornness to criticize my lodgings, and I didn't want her advice either, although she admitted it hurt her to think I was going to live in a house without my own private bathroom.

Later that day, a male friend jokingly suggested she could install a second bathroom for me in the co-op if it upset her that much.

I didn't explain that my mother had groomed me to be a writer, and set me in motion deliberately, the way you cock a rifle or a gun, and suddenly here I was in a ramshackle co-op about to live a life she couldn't understand.

Like many enthusiastic readers, she idealized writers and their creative lives. Until, that is, the day she and I heard the late Canadian author Robertson Davies give a talk. She was horrified when the author of the wonderful novels she loved turned out to be the pompous, self-satisfied man on stage laughing at his own jokes. I cannot bear another minute, she whispered. Despite her good manners, we stood up and pushed past the startled people sitting in our row, my mother apologizing when we stumbled over their legs on our way out of the auditorium.

The magic portal into a box-less world

1.

Newly divorced and still a new mother, I can hardly believe I've had the courage to go out on my own and search for a place where I can be myself. For the first time in my life, I've escaped my family's conservative ways, and I can no longer complain that the tradition box is holding me back. But there are no directions for me to follow about how I want to live. Most of the older women writers I know aren't good role models on how to be a mother and a fiction writer. They live alone and many of them are alcoholics. Their lives could be a portent of what's to come.

My new life feels secretly terrifying, as if a bomb has gone off and I'm driving away at top speed down a highway with no traffic signs, whistling past shuttered farmhouses and fields with blackened crops.

Putting aside my fears, I hurry down to the city's unemployment office looking for a job that will give me enough time to write fiction. Although I've been trained as a journalist, I don't want to be a full-time reporter because work like that will consume me. So I apply for a position as a tearoom waitress and as an assistant to a young filmmaker making a documentary about Portuguese fishermen.

I'm fired from the tearoom after a week. I'm slow-moving, the manager says. Clumsy, he means, and too much inside my head, although he's too polite to use words like that. He says I take too long to walk back and forth from the kitchen with the orders.

The job with the filmmaker works out. Jordan is seated behind a grand piano the afternoon I meet him in his gloomy downtown apartment. He doesn't stand up to greet me. He remains seated at the piano, the afternoon light falling on his serious young face.

Talking in a deeply hesitant voice, he tells me he has just inherited a fortune from a dead relative. He's taken a course on how to handle his inheritance, but he has difficulty organizing his time, and he needs an assistant. I explain that I'm good at organizing my time and I'll organize his. He seems relieved and begins to play a

Mozart piano sonata. I listen for a few minutes before realizing I've been dismissed. I tell him I'll report for work the following week and he smiles, his heavy-lidded eyes half-closed.

2.

It's spring 1974 when I move into the co-op. It's located in the heart of Toronto's Annex, a neighbourhood of huge, shade-giving trees and large brick Victorian houses. Our co-op isn't a mansion. But it's substantial. It was likely built for a prosperous WASP family by the developer Simeon Janes, who was transforming farmland in the 1880s into an elite residential area of the city.

My daughter's bedroom window and mine look out at the sheltering branches of maple and oak trees and the gentrified fronts of the houses across the street. Our co-op is rundown but none of the neighbours complain. That's because most of Toronto's left-wing urban activists live in my 'hood, including Jane Jacobs, who left New York for Toronto and was widely quoted as saying the Canadian city was a safer, more harmonious version of the Big Apple. In 1971, she helped stop construction on the Spadina Expressway, which had been designed to go through Toronto's neighbourhoods. This meant Toronto's core wasn't hollowed out by suburban migrations like many American cities had been, and its powerful urban lobby, led by Jacobs and, later, Mayor John Sewell, were determined to keep it that way.

For the past few days, I've been thinking about what a co-op like ours meant for artists and writers starting out on their careers. It shocks me to recall how little I paid to live in its capacious rooms, all with ten- or twelve-foot ceilings. It was part of the luck of my sixties generation. Most of us weren't carrying the huge student debts that come with college life now, and we could afford rooms or apartments downtown while we worked on our books and our theatre shows.

In my journal, I write about what I'm experiencing: *New windows, new views, the clothes in old closets no longer fit.*

Most of the tenants are a decade younger. A young artist named Tina befriends me and says everyone in the co-op likes having a mother and a child living in the house. She points out that she and the others will babysit for free if I want to go out in the evening. And soon enough Sam, or Sammy, as she is sometimes called, endears herself to the tenants by offering her bottle to anyone who comes into the communal kitchen while she's in her high chair. They're surprised by her generosity and they love her for it. When Sam is three, Tina and her friends will come to our rooms so Sammy can approve of their outfits before they go out. As a toddler, she already has a fashion sense.

The landlord lives a few houses down the street. He's a developer, and relations with him are often in turmoil. Someone at the co-op will hear a rumour that he's going to sell our house, and a delegation that usually includes me, as the older house member, will walk over to his place to negotiate with him. But he isn't selling. He's waiting, like many speculators, for housing prices to rise, which indeed they do and by then I'm long gone.

The cheap rents, along with lower food prices, leave us free to play-act the life of a writer or an artist in the centre of a metropolitan hub. I'm using the verb *play-act* because that's what many of us were doing—working on creative projects that bring us some notoriety without having to deal with the struggles of establishing a professional career.

But something else is going on without me realizing it. By chance, merely by taking two rooms in a downtown co-op, I've slipped through a portal into a world without boxes. Toronto's underground art scene in the seventies is an urban frontier whose practitioners are out to challenge conventions about the way art is made. They abide by different artistic rules because they make things up as they go along. Performance art explodes everything; it's pure chaotic creativity and it refuses to acknowledge boundaries. What could be more permission-giving for a woman like me, struggling with doing the kind of writing I want?

HERE'S HOW I became a performance artist:

At the co-op I move the collection of antique pine furniture bought on my reporter's salary into its living room. My collection includes a long refectory table from Quebec, six matching captain's chairs, and a comfortable sofa. The effect is like plastering Italian marble on plywood and I sit in the living room with its decaying Edwardian grandeur and daydream about the novels I'm going to write—one day. *One day* is the operative word. I have trouble getting started writing fiction. My training as a professional journalist who filed a story every day means I feel self-indulgent sitting at my desk without producing anything. So I strike a bargain with myself. Every morning, after I feed my daughter her breakfast of soft-boiled eggs in the co-op kitchen, I take her to daycare. Back at the co-op, I sign in at my desk.

During that time, I can't rearrange my bookshelves or talk on the phone. Those four hours have to be solely about fiction writing, even if I don't do any actual writing. I must be either thinking about writing, researching writing, making notes on writing, or writing. After a while, my morning ritual starts to feel natural.

In the early afternoon, I sign out and work on research for Jordan or write a freelance journalism story until I collect my daughter from daycare. Supper follows, and bedtime stories, which end in a recital of all the people in her life who love her. Can you tell me their names again, Mommy, she asks. I'm careful to include her father in the litany of family friends and relatives.

The late Hugh MacLennan is on my mind. During one of his office hours at McGill, he had inquired in a kindly voice why it was that I always handed in unfinished stories. I didn't know how to answer him, and now, emboldened by my new life, I'm determined to tackle my weird reluctance to complete my stories.

The voice of my inner critic shouts: *Isn't it because you're too lazy to finish what you started? Why can't you be more serious?* Then, one night in my bedroom at the co-op, five black-robed male judges appear in a dream. One of the judges points at me and shouts: *You can't fool me! You have no talent.*

In an exercise at my desk, I write out a dialogue with one of the judges. It's a technique I'm learning to handle my self-doubt. Once I begin questioning the judge he turns into my father, who says, after I press him, that I'm not spending enough time writing fiction. Now that I have deigned to listen to him, my inner critic admits I do have talent, but I need to write more. He speaks in a fatherly, concerned tone, and I can't help agreeing with him. Our dialogue goes like this:

Me: Why do you think I have no talent?

The Judge: Isn't it obvious?

Me: Not to me. Why do you say that?

The Judge: I worry about you, you silly girl.

Me: It's nice that you care enough to worry.

The Judge: Well, thank you, Susan. It's high
time you started listening to me.

Me: Your words mean something. Do you
really think I have no talent?

The Judge (in an affectionate paternal tone now):
Did I say you had no talent? I was trying to get
your attention because you're not writing much
fiction. You need to set aside more time to write.

Me: That's good advice.

The Judge: You have talent. You know that, don't you?

Me: Okay maybe. But I can't finish my stories.

The Judge: You're afraid of being judged. It's time to let
that fear go and start typing THE END. Good luck!

That conversation is enough to keep me going for a while, although I'm still writing poems and chunks of prose that don't turn into a polished story. My favourite poem is only a few lines:

I have more currents than a river, more sides than the
moon. Haven't you noticed as I walk towards you a
hundred-limb image constantly flexing and refolding?

Meanwhile, the co-op hums with the activity of its dancers and musicians, who are playing in indie bands or staging their own independent theatrical pieces. Some of them are helping me with the vegetable garden at the back of the house. It's a huge space walled in by a wooden fence.

One afternoon, while I'm doing some weeding, one of the young musicians asks why I didn't stay with my husband. I explain that my ex-husband and I have different values and want different things out of life. The young musician shakes his head grimly and says that man and woman belong together. Those were his words. *MAN AND WOMAN*. He's all of eighteen, and he sounds like an older member of my family who told me a wife should stay with her husband no matter what. Seething, I stalk off to make coffee and run into a young composer who is talking at the kitchen table with another member of the co-op. As I plug in the kettle, he casually asks me for a piece of my unpublished writing because he wants to incorporate it into a performance of his that will feature music he has composed on a computer. Later, when I go to see his show, I discover that he has reduced my prose to a minor element in his musical composition. But the theatrical experience is intriguing. I realize I can do what he does, except that I intend to build my performance around my words.

3.

Take off your glasses, the choreographer Margaret Dragu shouts at me during a rehearsal. And give me those papers in your hand. You *have* to be in the moment.

We're working on a show about my obsession with the late Barbara Ann Scott, a Canadian figure skater, and I don't have a clue how to do what Margaret says. Like many writers, I'm not a natural performer. I read my poetry in a stodgy, affected way, and people sometimes walk out. I secretly prefer to be in the audience. It's not until I begin teaching creative writing that I figure out how to be comfortable talking in front of a crowd.

Margaret's reputation as a performer was already legendary when a friend introduced us in the co-op kitchen. I was giving Sam her last bottle of the day, and as soon as Margaret and I began talking, I knew she was the one to help me with my first performance piece. It's a show I wanted to put on about a famous Canadian woman figure skater. But after I put Sam to bed, Margaret told me she wasn't interested. Why should I help you, she asked. For an answer, I put my cardboard carton filled with photographs, news stories, and my unfinished poems about the figure skater on the kitchen table.

Because women are expected to be perfect, I replied, and I want you to help me do a show that exposes how unfair this is.

Margaret continued to look doubtful, so I added: And because no one else but you can be the imago of Barbara Ann. She raised her eyebrows and shrugged. I don't know what that word means, she said.

Imago means the idealized image of someone, I replied. Barbara Ann represented feminine perfection when I was a kid, so I've created an imago of her for the performance.

Slowly and carefully, Margaret began looking at what was in my carton. Perhaps she was affected by the feeling of creative energy in the shabby kitchen, where so many similar conversations about putting on theatre shows had been held. Or maybe she was touched by the idea of a single mother doing performance art, but

after another hour discussing what such a show could be like, she
said yes.

IT DOESN'T TAKE us long to become friends. We share a passion for experimental work as well as an aversion to public success.
Her aversion has to do with her allegiance to her working-class
roots, while my experience growing up in a small town has made
me apprehensive about attracting envy and the accusation that I'm
"too big for my britches." (Cowardice on my part, a problematic
loyalty on hers, because going after material success will take her
away from her roots.)

When we meet, Margaret is twenty-two and I'm thirty. She's
studied with major modern dance choreographers in New York
City, and in Toronto she is part of a group of independent dance
artists who hang out at 15 Dance Lab, a performance space created by Miriam and Lawrence Adams, former dancers with the
National Ballet of Canada.

So that day in rehearsal, I know she's right when she takes off
my glasses and removes the papers in my hand. I need to stop pretending I'm not on stage and be emotionally present. To make it
easier for me, she's designed a nervous-gesture dance based on my
nervous gestures, such as scratching my nose and twirling my hair,
things I do when I feel anxious.

During these rehearsals, Margaret is also teaching me that the
messy, imperfect creative process holds the germ of what we need
to create a performance. Talking about what to call our show about
Barbara Ann Scott, she lists twenty possible titles.

When I complain that none of her titles work, she laughs. Then we will make another list, she says. And another one after that if we still don't get what we want.

Three lists later, we have the title for our show about the Canadian figure skater: *Queen of the Silver Blades.*

EXERCISES LIKE MARGARET'S list-making are a revelation. Despite my discipline, I tend to write fiction only when I'm inspired, naively imagining that good writers don't revise their work because their stories pour out of them in perfectly shaped sentences.

However, writing a novel means putting aside the usual judgments about what you're working on and surrendering to the act of creating something from nothing. When I was a girl, I knew how to give myself over to telling a story to my girlfriends. Now I have to relearn what I knew and resist the impulse to start analyzing what I'm writing when I'm writing it.

If I'm too critical while I'm working on a draft, I run into writer's block. Nobody needs their inner critic in the middle of creating something; it's like inviting a food critic to dinner when you're chopping onions. The inner critic will come in handy later on, when you're getting ready to serve your feast.

4.

I don't admit it to myself, although it's obvious: the figure skater Barbara Ann Scott is a stand-in for my mother. Barbara Ann Scott represented female perfection, as it was understood in the 1940s and 1950s. She was, at the time, the first and only Canadian to win an Olympic medal for women's figure skating. And she was celebrated not only for her skating prowess but because she dressed and acted in a ladylike manner. Our show about her is put on twice: a single performance at a Toronto church in 1975, for International Women's Year, and, a year later, a two-week run staged by Red Light Theatre, a feminist company, at a downtown theatre.

The first theatre version of our show features three slide shows, a slew of poems (some about female genitals that would be difficult to get published in today's literary climate), and several dance numbers, which include a routine by three male karate students whom we call the Thin Ice Follies Chorus. While the Thin Ice Follies Chorus execute their karate moves, I intone a poem into a microphone. It's meant to be an exorcism of Barbara Ann's style of femininity: *Become a blurry poem, Barbara Ann. We want print all that's left of you.*

One part of the show features a mash-up of a taped media interview with Barbara Ann's coach Sheldon Galbraith and Margaret, who plays a campy version of my imago, the idealized image that represents the figure skater to me. We've created her role to exorcize the repressive femininity of Barbara Ann's generation. Or so our thinking goes. In the mash-up, Sheldon and the imago discuss figure eights, the set patterns that a skater traces in crisp, immaculate circles. Figure skaters are judged for their precision in figure eights, and their technical proficiency makes a big difference to the skater's overall mark.

Their conversation is designed to demonstrate how women are taught to conform to the standards of feminine behaviour. It's no accident that Barbara Ann's coach said that women were better at doing the figure eights than men because they tried harder to be perfect. Very deeply rooted is women's desire to please, Sheldon Galbraith tells the imago in our theatre show. A female skater will take the punishment of the detailed demands of figure skating as long as she gets the objectives she seeks. Men are on more of an ego trip, but women are willing to take a little more mental abuse. In our mash-up of his real interview, Sheldon concluded with absolute assurance: This is part of female nature.

The show also features photographs of my Barbara Ann Scott doll, a battered toy with a cracked but still-smiling face. Most little girls back then had Barbara Ann dolls, with fine-spun golden hair and eyelids with long black lashes that clacked when you moved the doll's head.

I TRIED TO figure skate when I was small and failed. I was already tall for my age and somewhat un-coordinated, so the only move I could pull off was shoot-the-duck. The manoeuvre consisted of squatting down and sticking out one leg as you sped across the ice. But I couldn't twirl and twist the way Barbara Ann did, nor could I perform a move known as the figure skating spiral. It involves skating on one leg while raising the free leg behind your back, and it's similar to the arabesque in ballet. Needless to say, Barbara Ann executed it effortlessly.

In my hometown arena, there were dozens of little girls my age turning over on their ankles as they tried to execute these figure skating postures. My mother watched me from the bleachers, and when I said I didn't like figure skating she didn't try to talk me out of quitting.

5.

In 1975, *Queen of the Silver Blades* attracts respectable art house audiences and is written up glowingly in the Toronto newspapers as
an international Women's Year project. I purposefully don't invite
my mother to *Queen of the Silver Blades*. But my aunt Susan Cowan
insists on coming and, afterwards, she buttonholes me and says
I've made her realize she has to update her clothes and hairstyle
so she doesn't look like Barbara Ann. It's an endearing attempt to
overlook what one theatre critic called a character assassination of
the fifties generation.

One night, our ticket-taker tells us that Barbara Ann's relatives
have bought tickets for our show. He says they're excited to see
it. They must have wrongly imagined that it would celebrate their
family member. Our underground audience understands our feminist views, but we're not expecting older people to come, let alone
Barbara Ann's family. I peek nervously out from behind a curtain
and spot their eager faces staring up at us from the front row.

Inevitably, as Margaret and I begin doing our imitation of an
obscene caller, breathing heavily into the mouthpieces of two
black rotary telephones, there's startled whispering from several of
her relatives siting in the front row. Following the telephone scene
comes the whirling crotch slideshow, a photomontage that shows
Barbara Ann spinning faster and faster on the ice until the skating
outfit flies off her trim athletic body and she's naked. At that
moment, the Scott family rises to their feet and walk out.

No doubt they found our theatre show cruel, and there's no
denying that cruelty is part of our performance, although we don't
see Barbara Ann as a perpetrator of the values that tyrannize us as

women. We see her as a dupe of a patriarchal system exemplified by the Playboy notion that women should be clothed in skimpy outfits and serve men drinks.

AFTER WE PERFORMED our first show, in 1975, I talked a Canadian magazine into letting me do a feature about Barbara Ann Scott. The editors liked my idea of describing the skater's post-Olympic life and the impact of her style of femininity on me as a girl. In those days, I wanted to try out my ideas in as many different genres of writing as possible so I could learn what each had to offer. But the article on the skater wasn't only a theoretical exercise; an interview with Barbara Ann would provide rich material for the second Toronto production of the show that the photographer Mary Canary, Margaret Dragu, and I were working on with Marcella Lustig, the co-director of Red Light Theatre.

Armed with cameras and tape recorders, Mary Canary and I fly to Chicago to interview the five-foot-two skater and her husband, Thomas King, a former professional basketball player who runs the Chicago Merchandise Mart. They've never heard of our show, *Queen of the Silver Blades*, and they know nothing about performance art or the Toronto underground scene. It's another world from their Chicago life, and they receive us courteously, politely hiding their bewilderment over our scruffy hippy clothes and the things we say that suggest we aren't typical figure skating fans. In fact, the cultural divide between my generation and hers is difficult to bridge, and Mary and I are astonished at how old-fashioned she and her husband seem. They make our own mothers and fathers look modern.

Barbara Ann retired from skating after she married Tom in

1955, and she tells us her new job is looking after him and her two kitty cats, as she calls her pets. In their handsome Chicago apartment, I'm struck by the way she lightly dismisses the numerous skating trophies displayed on shelves. When I ask about them, she acts as if someone else has won them. It's clear she's wary of claiming the dedicated and exacting competitor she turned into on the ice. Is that an unconscious strategy—to refuse to own her accomplishments? I guess yes and feel a tug of sympathy and recognition. Most of the women I know, including myself, don't claim our accomplishments. It doesn't matter if it's cooking skills, academic marks, or athletic prowess. Talking about your success doesn't jibe with trying to be smaller and quieter than men. And it certainly doesn't fit the code of behaviour that women like Barbara Ann followed. That code was as uncomfortable as their girdles. Consciously or unconsciously, they believed it was a woman's duty to accept their female role without complaining.

6.

I've placed a framed poster about my show on Barbara Ann Scott above my desk. It's the size of a small print, although it's not easily overlooked. Its image shows the skater high in the air, her legs split in a stag jump, her form-fitting satin pants under her luminous skating costume fully exposed above the heads of tiny male figures that represent figure skating judges. The men are holding up scorecards on her performance while Barbara Ann sails far above them, smiling ecstatically and seemingly oblivious to the fact that the world is staring at her crotch. The title on the poster is the title of our show, *Queen of the Silver Blades.* Its saucy subtitle is an in-joke: *A Salute to the Vertical Smile.*

Until recently, I rarely looked at the poster of our show, which I'd deliberately hidden in a back room. A few years ago, at a literary retreat, an Australian writer brought up *Queen of the Silver Blades* and said how much he liked the poems with the title "Performance Ode" that appeared in *Descant*, a literary journal. I quickly brushed away his comments. The other writers at the retreat knew me as a novelist, and I felt weird about people bringing up some of my outrageous literary experiments as a performance artist.

To be honest, I've never come to terms with the shows we did about Barbara Ann Scott. The performances bristled with the ferocity of youth along with the righteous anger (and sometimes hatred) young women can feel towards their mothers, who, like good colonizers, can be overly zealous in policing their daughters. One of my first attempts at a short story, "Girls Against Spinsters," described the power struggles between young girls and boarding school matrons. That unpublished story turned into my novel *The Wives of Bath.*

So a few weeks ago, I retrieved the framed poster of the Barbara Ann Scott show from its hiding place and put it on the wall where I can see it while I'm writing. I look at it every day as I mull over the perplexing questions it raises about making art.

7.

In her book *The Art of Cruelty,* the American critic Maggie Nelson argues that cruelty has been a common feature in twentieth-century art, that it is linked to rupture, to revelation, even to revolution, and she says this style of art confronts customs and platitudes begging to be shattered. Nelson excels at opening up a discussion of difficult issues but she doesn't come to a moral conclusion about the value of cruelty in art, and I don't have a definitive answer either, except to say that satire needs a knife-edge to be incisive and at that time we had been heavily influenced by a popular seventies concept: the art of making familiar things strange.

We'd never heard of the late Russian critic Viktor Shklovsky, although we were using a technique he described called *de-familiarization*. It means de-familiarizing common things in a theatrical way in order to jolt people out of their traditional assumptions. So as far as we were concerned, the weirder and more daring our shows appeared the more chance there was of our audience rethinking their views.

We prided ourselves on playing with irony for serious political purposes—destabilizing irony, as the postmodern critic Linda Hutcheon called it—and how we used it had little in common with the ironic stance that nineties television shows like *Seinfeld* made popular. In order to make theatre a radicalizing experience, performance artists also tried to break down boundaries between the artist and their audience. We dared/hoped our shows would be a radicalizing experience.

Dance versus writing

A choreographer named Louise Garfield lives two bedrooms down the hall. She also puts on shows at 15 Dance Lab, and after *Queen of the Silver Blades*, she and I start collaborating on performances.

In our first show, *Dance Versus Writing*, we hit each other with foam baseball bats and argue about who is more pathetic: inarticulate dancers or writers out of touch with their bodies. Our audience cheers wildly.

Our show *Balloon Slices* features giants and dwarfs. In a note about the show, I write that it's "an exploration of size and power." Pressing her face into the vinyl surface of a gigantic weather balloon, Louise holds an imaginary, guilt-ridden conversation with her mother while I gambol over a floor strewn with my daughter's Barbie dolls, babbling like a two-year-old about Daddy coming home.

Our performance *Down and In* investigates the emotion of self-pity as romantic feelings towards the self. It goes on a tour that includes a show at the Detroit Institute of Arts. Wearing toques and scarves and skimpy halter tops and short shorts, we list our grievances while immersing ourselves in the courtyard fountain. As we moan about how much we hate winter the room goes dark. When the electricity is finally turned back on, we can't touch the microphones with our dripping-wet hands. The blackout wasn't in the plan, but it makes our performance even stronger because we truly feel sorry for ourselves.

Like so many of the shows with Louise Garfield, *Down and In* is the essence of burlesque.

Meanwhile, I'm continually asking myself: How am I going to write original novels that leave an impression on readers? On a wall in my room at the co-op, I've written my motto in black marker: *To astound, to entertain, and to make people think.* My aspirations were in sync with the way many of us in artistic circles dreamed that art, of all things, might be more powerful than

politics in changing the perceptions of our audience. In the chaotic and innovative seventies, maybe all of us were looking for
a magic lodestone. Something to hold on to that would move
us forward into our lives along with the hope for a fairer, more
thoughtful society. *And many of us are still looking.*

Life with a large body: a solo performance

The lights have been dimmed as I sit stripped of my clothes in a
large dance studio staring at my nude body in the floor-to-ceiling
mirrors on the studio walls. I've never done anything like the solo
performance I've planned for this evening. I'm going to spend the
night naked and alone in the dance studio so I can see myself from
different angles in the glass. I'm shivering as I make notes, and try
not to feel foolish about the assignment I've given myself.

I don't think of it then, but what I'm doing evokes the old
memory of burying myself in the sand by the polliwog pond, trying to hide the body that is causing me so many problems. Except
that now I am staring it down instead of trying to wish it away.
Will studying myself in the mirror for hours provide me with a
liberating insight? Will I learn what it means to live inside the
body of an oversized woman?

I'm doing the night in the dance studio during the two weeks
my daughter usually spends with her father, so it feels like I have
all the time in the world to make my body the subject of a project
titled *Getting to Know You.*

Only a few people, including a dancer at the co-op, know where
I am. I rented the studio from one of the dancer's friends. Nobody

calls or knocks at the door and of course there are no cellphones, so I'm cut off from human conversation unless I want it.

The alarm clock I brought with me ticks on. Nothing happens. No astonishing shift in perception swirls within me. I no more understand what being a large woman means than I understand my own femininity. In the morning, after a bad sleep on one of the studio mats, I write the beginning of a long poem. The poem documents the parts of my body that I see in the mirror, the endless legs and delicate breasts, the smallness of my head compared to my long torso . . .

Later, at a festival of women's writing at a Toronto university, I will take off my clothes and stand naked with my feet in two buckets of water, reciting the poem I began to write that night, called "True Confessions of the Female Organs." The room was packed and a friend had to man the door to keep people from interrupting my reading. But like all art, the poem will succeed in describing my experience but it can't solve the conundrum of living inside a large female body in a culture that likes women to stay small.

THE POEM I wrote and performed after the night I spent naked in a dance studio was one of hundreds of experimental pieces staged in the private communal party that made up Toronto's underground art scene. The list is long and included many artists who became my friends, like the writer Marni Jackson, who wrote the scripts for the Clichettes, a performance group that lip-synced popular songs; the groundbreaking video art by Vera Frenkel and Lisa Steele; Tom Dean and his prints, books, and monumental sculpture like *The Floating Staircase* launched in the Toronto harbour; choreographers like Elizabeth Chitty and Tanya Mars; John Massey's intelligent photo-conceptual art, along with the critic Peggy Gale, who is known for her thoughtful critiques of video art that had become popular in international art circles.

For each show, we write a press release and make a poster, and we distribute flyers about our performances in downtown restaurants and art galleries. Our shows rely on audiences having a long attention span, and the posters are sometimes better than the performances, which can feel thrown together at the last minute. The design of the posters is usually witty, and sometimes ingenious. In a poster created for a show based on a collection of my stories about northerners on tropical vacations, titled *Unfit for Paradise*, the lead actress stands next to a group of slender women wearing bikinis, a beach ball incongruously bulging beneath the cloth of her one-piece bathing suit.

General Idea, a trio of downtown conceptual artists, publish droll, stylized critiques of mainstream culture in their magazine, *File*; they are the co-founders of Art Metropole, the artist-run centre specializing in art books and publications; videos and prints. Their gallery, like the Peter Pan restaurant, is a community hub in Queen Street West, which is the downtown area that artist-developer Charlie Pachter is transforming into a fashionable address.

During these years, the performance art community is a Bohemian outpost like the one in Christopher Isherwood's book *Goodbye to Berlin* (later made into the film *Cabaret*). It offers the chance to do creative work instead of the stressful job of newspaper reporting. As a reporter, I once interviewed a sculptor who had put on a hazmat suit and facial visor for our interview even though he wasn't welding that day. It was my first inkling that many artists perform the role of an artist in order to establish their credentials. Fooling around with artistic identities is a huge part of the conceptual art scene, and their approach inspires me to coin a phrase—"The art of being fame-ish"—in order to describe the playful irony being expressed in their performances.

To become fame-ish, all you need is a grant to put on a show and the ability to draw a modest crowd. Arts grants are more available for books and theatre shows because there is less competition, and the world seems genuinely interested in what young people are doing. A journalist calls up a friend writing her first novel and wants to do a story about the work-in-progress. Pleased and slightly embarrassed, my friend puts the journalist off.

Most of the downtown dancers, painters, poets, sculptors, and artists I know perform in each other's shows, which are usually staged at artist-run centres designed to support their work. Many of these artists are mixing tropes and techniques from film, photography, and literature in an attempt to create a new kind of conceptual art that is obsessed with biography, perception, gender, and role-playing. Playing a role is preferable to a career or doing a job. Roles are more fun; they add spice to the performative nature of the lives of the artists, whose personal obsessions are exploited in the performances.

Unlike today's internet influencers, nobody in the scene talks about how many eyeballs their work attracts. Commercial success is associated with losing your artistic integrity because you must please a mass audience. So most of the artists are living modestly on part-time work like waitressing, and supplementing their salaries with grants and residencies.

A number of performance artists celebrate what makes them different. The late David Buchanan, for instance, wittily exalts his gayness in his piece *Del Monte Fruit Cocktails*.

I'm not fully aware of how permission-giving this kind of performance work will be for someone like myself, secretly concerned with being big. Not yet, but in time I'll come to think of many of these extraordinary pieces of original homegrown performance art as part of my unofficial PhD from the underground academe. Performance art is not only teaching me that I have the right to make art the way I like—it's giving me techniques on how to do it.

Canada lacks the megaphone of a country with a mass culture like Germany or America, and a large number of these experimental art projects resemble the efforts of the Wright brothers before they learned how to fly a plane off the sand dunes at Kitty Hawk. Their impact has vanished like footprints washed away by the ocean, a metaphor that would likely please some of the artists who were never very interested anyhow in monetizing their art. Conceptual art doesn't transform itself easily into a product that people buy, and most practitioners are more engaged with the art of being fame-ish than with starting a commercial career. Their philosophy is a relief for me because I was still exploring how to be a writer who does original work, so I could avoid worrying about the need to write the safe, consumer-friendly kind of books that publishers might prefer.

In his book on the seventies art scene, *Is Toronto Burning?*, the curator Philip Monk says the only people you'd see in the deserted area on Queen Street between Beverley and Spadina were winos or members of the underground art scene. According to Monk, our community was invisible except to those who sought it out and willingly learned its lingo. Although Andy Warhol and his collective the Factory had been influential in the sixties, nothing new and exciting was coming out of New York City after that, so Canadian conceptual artists were free to develop in their own way, and some of the underground artists I knew were getting an international reputation.

The tailored coat

A few months after I move into the co-op, my mother appears at the door, holding out a tailored tweed coat that she wants me to wear. She's taking me to get a cyst removed from my knee and she doesn't want me to be seen in public wearing unsuitable clothes. In a glance she takes in the overalls and cowboy boots I'm wearing that morning, and when I ask about the coat, she says nervously that she wants me to look my best.

As we stand looking at each other, I think of the family photograph of my mother with my grandmother when she was small. My grandmother is holding out a jacket for my mother to wear, and my mother is standing just outside my grandmother's reach. She stares at the camera with a look of rage and frustration, refusal inscribed in the muscles of her small body, while my grandmother looks on in surprise and bewilderment.

The photograph says everything about my mother's resistance to her own mother's will, just as I'm resisting the will of my mother.

My mother notices the newly vacuumed broadloom in the front hall and, grudgingly, she follows me into the gloomy living room where she stares in disbelief at me sitting on the couch I've brought from my former home. I try not to stare back. In her pale blue suit and Holt Renfrew coat, she looks out of place in the dark, untidy room.

She starts by filling me in on some news about my grandmother while I listen, waiting for her to say that I'm turning into my country-doctor father, who had no time for his family. She doesn't believe women should have a full-time career once they've had a child, and since I've left my marriage, she's started remarking as if speaking to no one in particular: "Doctors shouldn't have wives." Her pointed comment is aimed directly at me: *Ambitious writers like you, Susan, shouldn't have children.*

I never think to reply that wives should be able to be doctors too. I feel off balance with her and guilty about not sticking it out with my marriage. I'm always letting her down, it seems. The force of her disapproval feels almost as powerful as my drive to write novels. Transposed on the pages of my journal is a cold beautiful face. Its expression always says the same thing: not good enough.

Why do mothers exert such a powerful hold on their daughters? Is it because daughters grow inside their mother's bodies and our hearts beat in close, similar rhythms? Two women already entwined in an indisputable physical connection that doesn't happen with fathers and sons? No boy grows inside his father's stomach only to emerge as himself.

In an attempt to reassure her, I explain, Look, I'm alive, I'm happy, I have my lovely baby, I'm earning my own money, and I've started to do the writing I want to do.

I tell her all of us have a legitimate interest in experiencing a well-lived life and that we're not obliged to live up to other people's expectations. Well, I don't say it so formally, but that's the gist.

My mother doesn't respond to my comment about a well-lived life. She doesn't see any difference between healthy self-interest and selfishness.

In a few minutes, our polite conversation comes to an end, and my mother gets up and holds out the tailored coat again and asks me if I will please wear it to the hospital.

For a few seconds, our gazes lock. She looks hopeful. Then I sigh and shake my head. It's one of your prettiest coats, I reply. But the style is too conservative for me.

Dropping my eyes to avoid seeing the look on her face, I grab a well-worn jacket from a newel post in the hall and off I go with her to the hospital, determined not to play the part of the young matron she thinks I should be.

The zeitgeist is on my side

Fortunately for me the zeitgeist is on my side. Feminism is a powerful social force in the 1970s. The birth control pill is suddenly an option, after centuries of pregnant women dying from back-street abortions.

It's also the decade of the Watergate scandal and tennis star Billie Jean King winning the "Battle of the Sexes" match against Bobby Riggs, the gay liberation movement, the Roe v. Wade abortion law, the end of the Vietnam War, and the Shere Hite report debunking the vaginal orgasm. It was a time when women from my generation declared they wanted the same privileges as men. We entered the workforce by the thousands and demanded to be called by our own names. After I married, I had to fight to keep my professional byline with the personnel director at my newspaper. He mistakenly claimed it was against the law for married women to keep their maiden names. Our discussion was personal for him, and I refused to budge.

In those years, the social code was resolutely binary; it was before activists lobbied to include trans and non-binary people in the gender spectrum. Only two genders were acknowledged— male and female heterosexuals, and god help you if you didn't fit neatly into one of those boxes. (There you go—more boxes.) And here was a box as solid and confining as most of the boxes I had found myself in, and, just like the other boxes, at first I didn't know where I was.

Heterosexual men were the gold standard. I wanted to be successful, and the way to get ahead (or so I thought) was to act like a man. What did that mean? Be dominant. Don't listen to people who disagree with you. Put your work before the people in your life. If you're a woman, a shift in your behaviour is required.

It astonishes me to remember how hard I tried to act and think like how I imagined a heterosexual man acted and thought. Of course, my size makes it easier to fall into the trap of acting like a man because I sometimes pass as male if I'm seen from behind. Store clerks often call me sir by mistake, and then apologize when they see my face. The experience is slightly bewildering, as if I've been caught transitioning from one gender to another without the support of hormones, or medical advice.

Even now, all of us still live in the world heterosexual men have shaped, a world where femininity is an adjunct to a hyper-masculine definition of masculinity. Think of seatbelts in cars that cut across women's breasts because the designer had in mind a passenger with a flat chest. Think of subway stations with endless flights of stairs and the elevator (if there is one) far in the distance, an exhausting hurdle for young parents pushing children in strollers, as well as for heavy, disabled, or ill people. In a *New York Times* story titled "A Blind Spot" (October 18, 2022), Rachel E. Gross berates doctors for misdiagnosing women's sexual problems, a result of the fact that many medical schools still pay far less attention to female bodies, particularly their genitals, than to masculine bodies.

And on it goes. In his hit song from the 1960s, James Brown sings: "It's a man's man's man's world." No wonder many of us tried to adopt traditionally masculine habits of thought.

When I'm living at the co-op, the zeitgeist is strongly felt in Toronto's downtown. The city pulses with the energy of progressive change. Bell-bottoms and disco clubs are in fashion. Turbulent labour strikes are happening at RadioShack and Artistic Woodwork. Feminists and gay rights activists are lobbying passionately for their rights, and racial tensions will break out later, after the unprovoked shooting of three Black men.

And by the time I'm a mother, French author Simone de Beauvoir has already published *The Second Sex*, in which she argued that one is not born a woman but becomes one. Betty Friedan has diagnosed the malaise of unhappy female homemakers in her book *The Feminine Mystique*, and Kate Millett prophesied in *Sexual Politics* that marriage was a trap for women who wanted to lead independent lives. Andrea Dworkin had gone a step further and said sexual intercourse was an act of oppression against women.

I embrace much of seventies feminist thinking gratefully and willfully, although I'm careful not to mention my new boyfriend Christopher during political discussions with my activist friends. He has a small son, Tyler, who is my daughter's age, and the four of us enjoy spending time together. Christopher understands my ambition to write fiction because he grew up with an artist father. His liberal views appeal to me, but he belongs to the group of friends my ex and I used to socialize with. He's also a real estate developer, and that sort of work is frowned on in my left-wing circles.

More problematic is the fact that he's a man, and in some feminist circles, so the thinking goes, the only true feminists are lesbians, because their lives aren't dependent on men. However, I like men too much, and the extent to which I depend on relationships with them will be an issue later on when I take part in a diary project called "It's Not All Porn: A Treatise on Ethics."

My work for Jordan, the filmmaker, pays most of my bills. It involves writing letters on his behalf and arranging recordings at sound studios for the film's score, composed by a Portuguese friend.

My main job is setting up these recordings. The technicians at the sound studios don't take me seriously because I go to their meetings wearing overalls. So I begin showing up wearing an old tweed suit of mine with a skirt, with my long blond hair pinned back. Sometimes I wear a prim little hat. The technicians begin to treat me with more respect.

My outfit is a parody of what I imagine a businesswoman wears. It's part of the role-playing we are doing, and my campy suit makes Jordan and me laugh.

The dear-diary project

1.

As soon as I walk into my rooms at the co-op, I know Jordan has read the diaries. It's been eighteen months since I left my marriage and we're meeting to discuss the screenplay for his documentary on Portuguese fishermen, and he has come early. While I was out on a shopping errand, I left the diaries I'm exchanging in the mail with two performance artist friends out on my desk.

When I come back, he's sitting unnaturally still at my desk, holding in his hands the diaries, an expression of disbelief on his face. It occurs to me that I must have left the diaries open on my desk on purpose, because I'm secretly gleeful a man has set eyes on them.

Despite our despair and anger about our culture's conventional views of women, our diary entries are raunchy and joyful. They rebuke the notion of my mother's generation that women should be demure and ladylike.

One of Sandy's entries reads: *I want my lovers to adore me. I always want to be the other woman. Good one-night stands are fabulous . . . I want lots of pleasure. I want to give lots of pleasure . . . Mercy fucks are a sin against God.*

The same entry goes on to describe how she enjoys tying a man up and making love to him. In her case, it isn't an idle boast.

When Jordan sees that I'm not going to comment, he flops down on my bed, puts his hands behind his head, and stares dreamily up at the ceiling.

What are your friends like anyway, he asks.

I keep my eyes fixed on the screenplay in my lap. One of them will tie you up.

Tie me up! Oh my god, what kind of era am I living in?

Oh, I reply, still pretending I'm engrossed in the film script. She'll be very gentle.

Tie me up to what? he asks.

To chairs, anything that's available. And then she'll have her way with you.

A woman can't rape a man! he cries. I wouldn't get an erection.

You might, I tell him.

He considers my comment. Okay maybe I would. He laughs. Then he adds: I doubt it though.

He jumps up and starts to walk around my bedroom muttering and shaking his head while I keep annotating his film script. Our minds are doing somersaults. We're both aroused, and if I look at him directly, my composure will crack. I can hear Sandy's voice in my ear: *Tee hee. We're three bad little girls out to teach you a thing or two, mister.*

Finally, he stops pacing and gazes at me wonderingly. It's so intense, he says.

I know, I agree.

I couldn't stop reading it, he explains. At first I thought it had something to do with business . . .

He begins peppering me with questions, so I put down the screenplay and explain what my friends and I are discovering about our behaviour by exchanging the diaries in the mail.

I tell him each of us has a sexual ethic and I hazard a guess that this is likely true of most people. How did we figure this out? Each of us keeps acting out the same psychological script with our lovers that we unconsciously set in motion ourselves. We're both director and star of these roller-coaster sagas. The men are relegated to bit parts, and it's astonishing to discover our own agency in our romantic adventures.

Despite her tough exterior, Sandy sees herself as a rescuing angel, helping men be their better selves by listening to their problems and showering them with adventurous sex. In her case, this means love affairs with dozens of men, preferably men who seem as lost or confused as she often feels. Meanwhile, Leah is attracted to men who offer danger, and she has chosen an unreliable married man as her lover. This man is a member of her dance community, and the possibility of their affair being discovered terrifies and thrills her.

My ethic reflects my fear that I'm too big to be loveable, and I need to be eternally courted before I'm reassured that I am cherished.

I confide to Jordan that I secretly feel unsatisfied with my boyfriend Christopher, even though he understands my desire to write novels. I explain that I grew up with an absent father whose attention was on his work, not me, and I hunger to be reassured that I'm loved. I hope the man in my life will prove his love by asking me to marry him—even though I'm frightened of accepting a marriage proposal in case it means I won't have the time to write fiction.

Nevertheless, I hope Christopher and I will sooner or later live together with our kids. Auditioning for that future day, I often find myself playing the role of casual wife: I'm a better wife to him than I was to my husband. I read Jordan a diary entry that contains a satirical description of me trying to be all things to him, an intellectual companion and a domestic helpmate cooking steak and asparagus with Hollandaise sauce and dressed in my best jeans, my lips outlined with brown eyebrow pencil the way the fashion models used to do.

I longed to be as free as male artists and writers, but I was exactly like any other mother juggling a work-life balance. The credo of the age insisted artists should focus solely on their creative work. But how could I be so single-minded, with the demands of raising a child and the need to earn a living? And then write fiction on top of that? These conversations with myself always ended up in browbeating sessions. Either I was not giving my daughter enough time or I wasn't spending enough hours writing novels. Well, big girls don't cry, do they?

The truth is women are often in an impossible position between the demands on their time and their own wants and needs. As the critic Claire Dederer says, mothers feel like terrible people when they set aside childcare duties in order to write. Not that these mothers *are* terrible people, but they *feel* like terrible people because they are taking time away from their children to do something for themselves. I often felt like I was neglecting my daughter when I sat down to write fiction.

Meanwhile, Christopher likes the idea of a relationship where two people don't settle into roles. Having a wife would make him feel guilty, he says. I pretend to feel relieved, but secretly I want more reassurance that he loves me. While Jordan listens, nodding his head thoughtfully, I explain that I have no idea how to re-create a family with Christopher without compromising my independence. And my complex about my size still haunts me. Does my height engender the feeling that nobody can love me? Or am I just afraid of committing to another man after my divorce?

I tell Jordan that Christopher is a generous, fun-loving man who sometimes reads my work and makes suggestions about my stories. Later, he'll fund a short-lived independent press that fiction writer A.S.A. Harrison and I start with him. (The cost of distribution for a small press in a large country like Canada put an end to that project.)

Over and over again, I explain that I don't have a clue how to take my writing seriously and be a wife to a man. It's a conundrum. (It often still is.) At the time, women's magazines or books like *Sex and the Single Girl* by Helen Gurley Brown offered nothing but glib advice on how to have careers and still cater to men.

Meanwhile, in my diaries, I'm the neglected heroine while Christopher unknowingly plays the role of rejecting lover. Our relationship is more complicated than that, but I can't seem to alter my behaviour. Jordan smiles and nods in recognition when I admit that no matter how cleverly I analyze my behaviour, I'm still capable of working myself into a frenzy over feeling unloved.

When I admit I find our obsession with drama and romance in the diaries embarrassing, he says there's no reason to be embarrassed, because we're writing about the truth of our feelings.

Afterwards, I stand at the window of my room in the co-op and watch him stroll home under the flowering chestnut trees. A sexual attraction simmers between us, a sense of possibility that if he weren't my boss and if I wasn't seeing Christopher, we might hook up. Once, he left me a short note when I was out. It said simply, "I love." The note didn't say whom he loved, but I guessed he was expressing his appreciation over how much I helped him. I never responded, and now that he's ambling away, his hands tucked thoughtfully behind his back, a nice-looking young man in suede trousers and a matching suede jacket, I feel a jolt of guilt for tantalizing him with the confidences in our diaries. I played with him, daring him to object or be horrified, and all through it, he was a kind listener who seemed to genuinely want to understand what was motivating us.

2.

I'm glad I didn't tell Jordan about our sexual assignments.

What sexual assignments? you might ask.

Before I talk about the assignments, let me explain that working for Jordan wasn't turning out the way I expected. Although I successfully negotiated several recording contracts for the young filmmaker, he often refused to sign them. He didn't mind when I complained that he couldn't make a decision during a negotiation. Instead, he would turn my way and say, for once his sleepy eyes wide open: Sue, this is just the way I am.

I was startled by his honesty. Perhaps he learned to talk openly about himself in his therapy sessions. But I'm beginning to understand that he and I aren't alike.

I assumed we worked well together because we were both open to new ideas. Startlingly open. My first reaction is always to mull over a new idea as a real possibility before I identify its flaws and move on to reject or accept it.

It seems I need to *feel* each stage in my thought process before I make a decision. It's an instinctive way of working things out, and my method can be frustratingly slow, but I'm committed to taking action on my writing and my artistic projects, which wasn't the case with Jordan.

His openness to possibilities stops once he lets the possibility sit within him. He doesn't move to a decision like me but stays in limbo, always *about* to make a decision but never acting on it. I'm finding it hard to work on a project that has almost no chance of being made. If I'm going to work for money I need to feel I'm doing something useful and not wasting my time indulging the whims of a trust fund kid. He reminds me of Oblomov, the protagonist in a Russian novel with the same name. In the story by Ivan Goncharov, the young aristocrat rarely gets out of bed, and then only to move to a nearby chair.

During one of my pep talks about why Jordan needs to sign a recording studio contract, he gives me a faint smile and says to a friend listening to our conversation: Susan has her own creative life, you know. She's a writer and, you'll see, one day she will publish a book.

He's able to recognize the creative potential in me at a time when I'm struggling with my confidence, but he isn't able to act on that possibility for himself. As far as I know, he has never made his documentary film.

Just the same, it must be obvious by now that I'm avoiding telling you about the assignments. It's always disconcerting for a feminist to admit to being obsessed with men and sex.

The assignments

1.

The assignments are straightforward. The three of us will inflict on predatory, insensitive men the same callous and disrespectful treatment they dish out to women.

Sandy says we will be like three Wonder Women/Robin Hood comic book heroines out to work over the bad guys—all those creeps who have hurt our fellow sisters. We love her idea that goodness is on our side. We can still go to heaven. Thank god.

In my rooms at the co-op, we come up with three assignments. I'm to seduce a womanizing male poet and treat him like dirt.

Sandy is a singer whose task is to seduce a cocky young male singer from the Maritimes with a large female following, tell him she loves him, and then dump him without an explanation.

Leah, a dancer, is to rendezvous with an arrogant dance critic known for heartless love affairs and cruel newspaper reviews; she will make love to him, and leave after telling him he's a terrible lover.

We want our assignments to bring retributive justice to the men who cause women personal distress. We assume the assignments will be effective because the men we know don't like to be singled out as sex objects. When they're treated as prey, or summarily dismissed after sex, they act bewildered and disbelieving, as if the universe has pulled a fast one by switching around the power dynamic.

SANDY IS A pretty woman with a lithe body and short, spiky blond hair. She makes the male musicians in my co-op nervous because she eyes them lasciviously, checking out their bodies, sometimes making appreciative sounds with a suggestive flick of her tongue. I'm titillated by her behaviour, even though I know from her diaries that she feels more vulnerable than she lets on. She's deliberately using the persona of a male punk rocker. It's her way of feeling the same confidence we imagine powerful men feel. When she tells the guitar player who lives on the first floor that she wants to fuck him, he rolls his eyes in fear. She presses him, and he agrees half-heartedly.

He hides from her when she arrives for the assignation. I know what he's doing because he took me into his confidence. I don't want your friend treating me like a piece of meat, he complained. When she appears at the co-op, newly bathed, her messy blond hair washed and set, I'm the one who has to tell her that he isn't up for their rendezvous. Sandy shrugs it off.

I set up my rendezvous with the womanizing male poet on a Saturday afternoon when Samantha is with her father. On that weekend, however, her father is sick with the flu, so she stays home with me. She's still a toddler, and I decide to seduce the poet while she's having her nap in the next room.

He walks into my rooms at the co-op, a reedy young man with red hair and a permanent sneer. He bows and preens as he compliments me on the sorrowful poems about divorce that I've scribbled on my bedroom wall. His ghostly white skin reminds me of grubs found under a log, and for the first time, I wonder if I'm capable of pulling off the assignment when I'm not attracted to him. But it's too late. I've given my word.

I asked him over on the pretext that I need advice on my poetry, and he was eager to comply. He's known for seducing vulnerable young women who are starting to write poetry and then coldly dumping them. His MO is suffused with cruelty: he critiques the woman's artistic work, love bombs her, and then discards her, along with her poems or her acting, like a bag of rotting garbage.

He's been described as well-endowed, and noting his reputation as a seducer, a counterculture newspaper referred to him affectionately as the Golden Cock.

I begin by lighting the fire and then pouring us both a glass of red wine while he starts reading a sheaf of my poems.

In the next room, my daughter starts to cry. I wait for her to fall back to sleep but there's no use. She's upset. Apologizing to him, I pick her up and bring her in to join us. She's only eighteen months old and she can't talk, but she points at him and then points at me, her face bright with curiosity. It's as if she senses what I have been planning. He laughs and says, Quite possibly.

So there it is: a gesture of approval from the two of them for what I'm planning. A moment later, she begins to cry again. Once more I try to comfort her, but she rages and screams as if she is morally disgusted by my deviousness. He's sitting beside me on the bed, looking at her, and when I hold her up for a burp, she spits a long trail of smelly yellow vomit down his shirt and trousers.

He flees to the washroom to remove the vomit from his clothing. He says his clean white shirt is ruined, and I give him one of my T-shirts to wear. The flirtatious tension between us vanishes and in a few minutes, he's gone. My attempt to take revenge on him for his malicious treatment of vulnerable women is a flop. It turns out my daughter is the one, not me, who gives the Golden Cock a few distressing moments.

A FEW DAYS later, I learn that Leah has failed her assignment with the dance critic. That comforts me. Only Sandy manages to have sex with the young singer, and not just once but twice, on two separate summer evenings.

They meet in Halifax, and on their first night, it's like a summer romance, Sandy writes in her dear-diary letter. Maritime singer meets city-slicker punk rocker. As they walk and neck in a park, she suggests they go to his house instead of hers. He's shocked and hurt and the brooding look on his face reminds her of the actor Gene Kelly. In bed, he's shy, and she does her routine of the kind femme fatale who rescues men from their troubled lives. *Pleasure,* she writes in her diary to us. *Had no one ever done those things to him, the poor boy! Do you like this? And this? Does it feel like heaven or what?* He seems overjoyed, but when she says she needs to leave at four in the morning, he looks at her the way she looks at her married lovers when they leave her at odd hours.

On the second night, Sandy and her singer dance and sing in the downtown streets to live music. The crowd circles around her. Men send her flowers and beer as she belts out a Janis Joplin song, and her young lover cries, Sing for me, Sandy, sing again! Then it's five in the morning and she says she has to go back to THE OTHER MAN (Sandy's caps). He looks hurt. He shouts goodbye from the back of his van. She feels guilty as they make a date to see each other the next day.

On the third night, she is supposed to drop him—hard. Sandy's evening starts off badly. He confesses he's the type of person who prefers failure to success. He believes that many men would rather be done wrong by a woman than find a woman who loves them.

In short, Sandy is doing him wrong. He clicks his tongue and looks like he might cry and Sandy feels awful because he seems so sad. She can't bring herself to finish her assignment and say I love you before she drops him.

Sandy signs off her diary, promising to be tougher. She didn't expect her targets to turn into emotional mush after sleeping with them, and she has no interest in picking on sensitive men.

A YEAR GOES by. With the approval of my two women friends, I try and fail to sell excerpts of our journals to a Canadian magazine. I explain that their content challenges feminist assumptions that women shouldn't be obsessed with men, but the editor says the excerpts are too sexually explicit for a family magazine. Next, with my friends' approval, I write a short piece of literary fiction based on the experience of the diaries. It uses the title we've given to our project—"It's Not All Porn: A Treatise on Ethics"—and it's published in a literary journal.

During this time, Leah has moved to San Francisco and shocked Sandy and me by working as a female escort who sometimes has paid sex with the men. Sandy is taking on extra singing gigs and seeing a man who says he doesn't love her. Her diaries sound desperate instead of playful. She seems overwhelmed by her unhappy feelings.

Leah is the only one of us who appears joyful. She boasts that her job as a sex worker gives her power over men. She's still high on the kind of anger that seeks payback, while Sandy and I don't have the will to do more assignments. We thought we would feel our own power by mistreating men, but there is something creepy and mean about our project. Revenge feels petty and less pressing; it doesn't offer a political solution, only more emotional pain all round.

On a visit back to Toronto, Leah meets us for a reunion lunch at Mars Food, a downtown Toronto diner. It's famous for its French toast and a sign that reads *Just out of this world.* Halfway through her soup, Sandy remembers leaving a man tied to her bed. She throws money at us for the bill and disappears.

While we finish our lunch, Leah talks about her work as a female escort.

I'm in control when the guy pays for sex, she says, giggling as she munches on one of the restaurant's famous home-baked muffins. You should try it.

She beams when I say I wouldn't dare. She has outdone both Sandy and myself in the assignments. Her sexual ethic is danger, and she has taken on the most dangerous assignment of all: working as a prostitute.

2.

Almost fifty years have gone by since we exchanged our diaries, and I haven't seen Sandy for a while. Just a few days ago, on a research trip of mine, she and I meet at a Halifax café near the waterfront. It's a warm September morning and the nearby tourist shops are coming to life.

The busy coffee shop has mind-boggling choices, everything from chai lattes and Americanos to delicate teas with unrecognizable names. I look closely at my old friend. She's aged and making no attempt to disguise it. Her bedraggled blond hair is a faded grey. She wears no lipstick, no eyeliner, nothing to disguise the face that many older women like myself have now, faces that are no longer plumped up with estrogen but present their owner to the world— unvarnished, stripped back to their essential bone structure and complexion.

I love her high cheekbones; the sleepy, hooded eyes that don't miss a trick; the laughing mouth whose lips curl in an ironic smile when she's talking about something she thinks is unjust.

I look older too. Certain angles reveal gravity at work, and I'm startled when I see myself in unposed photos on my iPhone.

Sandy tells me she still feels distressed about the way our assignments ended. She feels guilty that Leah kept on with our mission by doing sex work. That was never what she wanted for Leah. I point out that Leah stopped hooking and moved permanently to dance in San Francisco before vanishing from our lives.

Sandy isn't comforted. She says she knew that Leah was competitive and she should have been careful about encouraging her. Because Leah could never resist going one step further than Sandy in our assignments.

That sounds right, although at the time I missed their competition to see who could be the most outrageous, the most sexually provocative, the most daring and brave. Sandy points out that she wasn't as brave and daring as she pretended to be, and she thinks it's damaging when your outside projects confidence and conviction to the world while the inside of you is in turmoil.

I'm chagrined because I admired her courage and I wasn't aware of just how deeply she suffered.

She says it's hard to know what's real when you're young and trying out stuff. She thinks we were naive to try to act like men. It was how we thought you acquire power and agency, but real power and the ability to achieve your personal goals grows out of the skills and the wisdom that come with experience. As she talks, it suddenly becomes clear that our assignments were more about impressing each other with our bravery and daring than wreaking havoc on men. They were proof of our friendship bonds, an undertaking like the ritual of cutting our little pinkies as kids and mingling the blood on our fingers so we could call ourselves blood sisters.

You can't really fake it until you make it, she says, clasping my hand across the table. The tender moment passes, it's time for me to go to the airport, and Sandy and I hug as if we won't see each other again. And at our age, there's always a possibility that we won't.

Sometimes feminism is just another box

1.

Rereading the diaries back in Toronto, I'm touched by our longing to have what we thought all men had—power and authority and the freedom to act without restraint along with the ability to escape consequences. An idealization if ever there were one. How many men really feel capable of this? Isn't this idealization dependent on a specific concept of maleness: wealth, whiteness, health, and heterosexuality?

It was as if my friends and I were trying to fit who we were as women inside the outline of a male paper doll, not realizing our emotional make-up and thinking apparatus were unlike what that outline represented.

In our diaries, we were preoccupied with men and our sexuality, and our passions set us against the feminist ideology of the times, which downplayed the importance of relationships in women's lives. Women like us who were romantically interested in heterosexual men were often dismissed as lipstick feminists.

However, the three of us didn't exchange the diaries with the idea of critiquing seventies feminism. Our project had been a genuine attempt to slip through a crack in the wall to a world where we hoped to gain personal and artistic autonomy and still be loved for ourselves. The diaries were crucial information, the time in my life when I first learned patterns, and that if I stayed in the same old dormant state of mind, it would be possible to amuse myself on Channel 2 forever. I remember how shocked I was to face my urge for security—my sexual ethic of marriage to the nth degree. I was under the misguided impression that freedom meant discounting my personal needs and feelings.

In the past, femininity, with its suffocating social controls, has been a dilemma for many women in a way that traditional masculinity hasn't been for most men. And feminism, with its political values, its evolving customs and beliefs, has been an effective strategy for women to get their rights recognized. However, feminist moralism can also be just another uncomfortable, tight-fitting box. It, too, can expect women to obey a rigid code of behaviour that denies their personhood along with the personhood of others, and in time, its heavy moralizing may seem overblown and even absurd.

During the seventies, many feminists like myself saw the family as a trap, and historically, the traditional family has limited women's freedoms. Then along came Generation X, my daughter's generation, who decided they wanted careers and husbands and babies; they had no interest in going through the painful divorces that my generation experienced. Instead, they were intent on re-creating the family so it works for them, and large numbers of that generation even took their husbands' last names.

2.

After I put the diaries back in my filing cabinet, it occurs to me that there is something unsettling about the way we couldn't see our own personal power. Instead, we portrayed ourselves as suffering heroines because, like many women, we were titillated by the seductive pleasures of female masochism. We were fooling around with tragedy, lured by the power of being a female victim, as if we agreed with the American poet Edgar Allan Poe's famous quote: "The death of a beautiful woman is, unquestionably, the most poetical topic in the world."

The appeal of victimhood came with a sexed-up seventies aesthetic in many popular films. Everybody knows this kind of imagery: Gorgeous women dying in shockingly violent ways. Skinny fashion models contorting their bodies in unnatural poses. Women draped seductively across cars in commercial ads. Ravishing victims were everywhere, and the lure of victimhood let us off the hook; we didn't need to take responsibility for ourselves, even though the diaries proved we had a hand in creating our personal circumstances. We often preferred to be hard done by, the injured party who exaggerates their helplessness in situations in which we were far from helpless.

Put simply, we struggled to accept our agency even though we weren't powerless. It would have been advantageous to acknowledge our strengths, but we couldn't see our own power at the time, and demeaning cultural attitudes to women were likely one of the reasons. Underestimating who we were affected the way I looked at my size too. I noticed only the drawbacks of being big and not the confidence it gave me in my physical presence and the authority that can come with that.

In my dear-diary entry dated August 30, 1976, I wrote: *I still don't understand our addiction to men and how did you put it, Sandy? Our infinite capacity to get hurt . . . I feel more vulnerable than my boyfriend. He takes our separations naturally and for me, they are a bit painful and bewildering . . . Sometimes I think men are a fringe activity. A weird part of our work, an ingredient in a bigger game and I wonder if another ingredient could be substituted as easily. I guess this is what Leah meant when she talked about the way we romanticized suffering in our diaries. Is it possible that men are all things to us? Part of our work . . . part of our emotional well-being. And then a yummy delicacy—oysters, bread, chocolates—everything.*

The single-mother box

Some people do drugs in order to have transcendent experiences, but instead of taking LSD, for half a decade in the 1970s I was living in the exalted world of performance art, a world of pure, sublime, luminous creativity whose citizens feel no limits except the limits of their imagination. However, the zeitgeist is shifting by the end of the decade towards a more material state of being. Women have started wearing power suits with padded shoulders to their office jobs, and kitchen islands made of marble or granite are becoming popular. The arts grants have become harder to get and my friends in the conceptual art community are starting to look for other sources of income. I'm in the same boat, so I stop cobbling together a precarious living from grants, journalism articles, and part-time work, and, together with two freelance writers, create the ABS Company, a publicity firm that sells our skills to an educational television network. We write press releases for the network, and the three of us rotate in and out of the same job for three months at a time.

When I start my new job, I write to Sandy and Leah in my diary: *This is real life, full stop.* I buy myself a pair of new shoes, cut my hair in a new style, clean out my two rooms in the co-op, rearrange my kitchen shelves, sort my daughter's clothes, help Christopher fix up a bedroom for his son in his house.

Every morning, as I join the crowd on the subway, heading north to the educational television network, I feel as if I'm descending a mineshaft only to crawl out at the end of the day with my creative powers in tatters, knowing I have sacrificed the time I needed to write fiction.

I don't think of it at the time because I'm so busy, but being a single mother is a box too, and a box that is restricted by the nature of what you have to do. My daughter spends two weeks at a time with me, per our joint custody arrangement, and it's a time when I will be all things to her—her mother, her father, her nursemaid, and companion. The single fathers I know hire housekeepers, and some of the women with office jobs do the same thing, but that requires a higher level of income than mine. If I have an hour to myself at night in the co-op kitchen to think and daydream about a novel, I feel lucky. I give her breakfast, drop her at daycare, work all day, pick her up after work, feed her dinner, put her to bed. When Sam returns to her father, it takes me a while to get used to her absence. I'm too disoriented to plunge quickly back into my writing, although I've been longing for endless hours to spend on it. Two weeks go by and, just as I'm getting used to life without her, she's back and the cycle starts all over again. Two weeks with me, and two weeks with her dad, and round and round it goes. Usually, I'm too tired to do much except stare blankly at the shadow of Samantha's skates dangling from the kitchen doorknob.

One evening, taking a cab home from the television station with some male producers, I listen as they start complaining that their wives are stopping them from writing great novels. I order the cab driver to pull over. Your wives take care of you, I snap as I jump out of the taxi. Nobody takes care of me. High on self-righteousness, I walk the thirty blocks home to my Annex co-op, where I type up fifteen pages of new writing.

Most of the publicists employed in the Information Department at the educational television station where I worked were writers like myself, and they were encouraging about my fiction. I'd started my first novel about the giantess Anna Swan, and my boss, an old reporting colleague named Pat Annesley, used to ask, How's the book going? When I said I had bad days, she would add, You have good days too, don't you? And if you're having good days, then your writing is coming along the way it should.

Drawn by the good salaries at the network, all of us spent our days pounding away at our electric typewriters in cubicles with doors you were able to close for privacy, (there were no open-plan offices then). As members of our ABS Company, we were an anomaly at the network because we didn't want to be there full-time, even though the job offered government pensions and benefits. The other two writers and myself were interested in using our lucrative salaries to buy us time to write.

Doing our job was like living inside the Hollywood movie *9 to 5.* It was mostly women rolling out press releases extolling a new documentary series, or stories for TV guides about programs like *The Education of Mike McManus,* which starred an ex-priest who had become a television personality after leaving the priesthood to marry a woman.

And mostly men were the television producers. They had their offices a floor below the Information Department. This led to compromised power dynamics where the men were constantly telling the women what to do, as if they were their personal secretaries or old-fashioned wives. A documentary filmmaker liked to verbally abuse the women information officers. One afternoon, it was my turn. I went over the newspaper journalists I'd approached on his behalf, listing their reactions to his show. But he kept berating me for not trying hard enough, and I became more and more frustrated over the fact that he wouldn't listen to what I was saying. His voice grew louder and louder until he was shouting in my face, and without thinking about what I was doing, I grabbed him by the collar, opened the door, and threw him out of my office. I've had enough of your complaining, I shouted while he lay sprawled on the hall floor. He picked himself up and scuttled away. Slowly, the doors to the other offices opened and women poked their heads out. Did we hear what we thought we heard? one of them asked.

Her face expressed disbelief. When I answered yes, the women cheered. The next day the man apologized and sent me flowers. Today, he would probably charge me with assault, and he might win his case.

The box with a bogey-woman

1.

The name of my old bogey-woman, Anna Swan, has floated up to me in a dream, and after beginning a short story about a large woman living in a castle, I realize a short story can't accommodate all the things I want to say about exceptional height in a woman, so I've decided to write a novel with Anna Swan as the heroine. I grew up in her shadow, and her personal history seemed to belong to the frightening world of my father's medical textbooks. In order to face the terror she inspired I would have to coax her out of a dark hiding place in my mind.

But I'm ready, oh, am I ready, to stare down the giantess who has haunted me ever since my ex-husband brought up her name when we were teenagers. In a rush of enthusiasm, I purchase a short book by Maritime historian Phyllis Blakeley titled *Nova Scotia's Two Remarkable Giants*. The 1970 book tells the life stories of Anna and the better-known Nova Scotia giant Angus MacAskill, who stood seven foot nine. He was then the tallest non-pathological giant in the world (meaning a pituitary tumour didn't cause his growth).

Most accounts of Anna's life exaggerate her height. At his show-place, the American Museum on Broadway, Barnum advertised her as "The Biggest Modern Woman of the World." Her height was seven feet six inches, although he lied and boasted that she was eight feet one inch.

However, the boastful word *biggest* in her billing wasn't far off the truth because she weighed 418 pounds.

Blakeley had been impressed by Anna's intelligence, and her scholarly book spoke about Anna's heart-warming story as Canada's only giantess who rose from humble beginnings to world renown.

Born in Tatamagouche, Nova Scotia, Anna began her life in a crofter's shack. According to Blakeley's account in the *Dictionary of Canadian Biography*, Anna was four feet eight inches tall at the age of five and weighed over one hundred pounds.

Fortunately for her, she didn't suffer from acromegaly, the condition that thickens the bones of a giant's face and limbs, and she looks attractive in her photographs.

One of her descendants, George Swan, told me that Anna's brothers and sisters resented the special treatment Anna received as a girl. She was too big and clumsy to work with them in the fields, and she stayed in the shanty wearing new dresses (because her clothes needed to be specially made) while her siblings had to be satisfied with hand-me-downs. Anna's pituitary abnormality wasn't shared with her family, who were all of average height. George Swan's height was average too.

In her teens, Anna was sent to teacher's college in Truro, where children followed her on the street and taunted her about her size. She lasted a few months before going home. Her family had no idea what to do with her. She was the third of thirteen children and the Swans were poor, so occasionally they exhibited their daughter at fall fairs to make extra cash.

Then P.T. Barnum's agent heard of the giant girl living in the bush, and in 1862, the agent persuaded her family to let Anna leave her hamlet in Nova Scotia and exhibit herself at Barnum's American Museum in New York City. She later left Barnum and went on a speaking tour of the British Isles. On the ship going over, she met the Kentucky giant Martin Van Buren Bates (1837–1919), who was four inches shorter than she was. They fell in love and she married him in a London cathedral. Queen Victoria gave them two giant gold watches as wedding presents. In 1873, she and her husband, the Kentucky giant, retired to a giant farmhouse they built in Seville, Ohio.

2.

When I sit down to write Anna's story, my humiliating experiences about my height help me understand the suffering she went through.

To compensate for her size, Anna dressed like a dignified Victorian lady, in bespoke gowns with billowing skirts supported by a sturdy framework of undergarments. The design of the dresses was taken from a popular fashion publication of the day called *Godey's Lady Book*. Anna followed their fashion guidelines in a painstaking (and hopeless) attempt to look "normal."

Anna's struggles with her femininity were on a different scale than mine, and her great sadness was her failure to produce healthy children like other women. Her first child, a girl, was stillborn in London, England, on May 19, 1872. The baby was twenty-seven inches long and weighed eighteen pounds. Her second child, of indeterminate sex, was born January 18, 1879, after an exhausting three-day labour. The child lived for eleven hours before it died. It weighed twenty-three and three-quarter pounds, with a breast measurement of twenty-four inches and a head circumference of nineteen inches.

To compensate for my height, in my school essays I had developed a pontificating prose voice that rambled on brightly about how much I liked being tall. I called this pontificating voice my spieling voice and I gave it to the giantess Anna Swan in my novel. Another tall woman, Toronto editor Louise Dennys, who stands five foot eleven in her stocking feet, bought the book for publication and helped me successfully shape Anna's story. The first edition of *The Biggest Modern Woman of the World* was published in 1983 and it has had many international editions since, including a recent publication in Portugal.

I don't tamper with the basic biographical facts of Anna's extraordinary life in the novel. But that meant I had to keep her giant husband in my story even though Martin Bates was a notorious bully who thought nothing of spitting tobacco on people's heads while he stood in the lineup at the post office.

In my novel, Anna falls in love first with the Maritime giant Angus MacAskill, who was known for feats of strength such as lifting a ship's anchor weighing twenty-eight hundred pounds. Their relationship doesn't work out in my book, and in real life Anna probably never met Angus, who was much older. But at least in my version of her story, she experiences love from a kind, more sympathetic man, and she also gets her own back at Barnum by instructing him on how to behave in the company of giants:

Do not ask, How's the weather up there? Or talk
    about good things in small packages.
Do not expect Giants to carry you when you can walk.
Do not climb to the top of a Giant's head to
    make yourself feel important.
Do not boil giant flesh for bones to make
    bridges, even in your imagination.
Do not kill Giants and steal their treasures.
Do not bring Giants gifts or take them out to the
    park because it is Be-Nice-to-a-Giant Week.

And so on.

Circus giants and the umbrella dance

A university experience was helping me write my novel about
Anna. At McGill, I dated a student named Michael, who was
five foot seven. Michael and his two extremely tall male friends
enjoyed turning daily activities into theatrical events, whether it
was directing downtown Montreal traffic in a top hat and tails or
phoning an expensive restaurant in old Montreal with the news
that ambassadors from an Eastern European country were coming
there to dine. The unsuspecting staff at the restaurant unrolled a
red carpet for Michael and his two friends, who were dressed in
red ambassadorial sashes and speaking gibberish that the French-
Canadian waiters couldn't understand. My girlfriend Nancy and I
accompanied them, secretly worried that all of us would end up in
jail, but the three men pulled it off with their usual flair.

They had perfected a routine called the Umbrella Dance, which they used to disrupt stuffy college parties. Nancy and I would take centre stage on the dance floor, a signal for the three men to raise black umbrellas and caper around us. Soon the crowd stopped dancing to watch and clap.

Our audience expected me to be with one of the six-foot-four college boys, but as the Umbrella Dance spun to a close, Nancy (who stood five foot four) ended up in the arms of one of the taller men while Michael tilted me back in a seductive pose and kissed me. Afterwards, he and I walked off the dance floor holding hands while our audience watched with their mouths open.

It was my first inkling that I could play with my size, that I could use my height as a theatrical tool to get attention. As Anna Swan discovered, there are benefits that come with extraordinary height. And many giants handle the trauma of being big by becoming an entertainer. When you get lemons, make lemonade.

Anna Swan's husband, Martin Van Buren Bates, had made a living as a circus giant after his experience fighting for the South in the Civil War. Then there was Eddie Carmel (1936–1972), the Jewish giant who posed next to his short parents in the famous photograph by Diane Arbus. He was, by turns, a stand-up comic, a rock 'n' roll singer, a writer of limericks, an actor, and a giant at a carnival sideshow. Before him came show business giants in England like Charles Byrne (1761–1783), a gentle, likeable man who could light his pipe from a street lamp.

The parents of the Dutch giantess Trijntje Keever (1616–1633) exhibited their giant daughter, nicknamed "De Groote Meid," at carnivals before she died of cancer at the age of seventeen. Advertised as a giantess over eight feet tall, she is depicted in an oil painting as a beautiful girl holding a rose in one hand and a fan in the other and dressed in the fashion of the times: a gown with a square white-lace collar that stood out from her broad shoulders like a small dining room table covered in white linen.

By the twentieth century, the prestige of celebrity giants had dimmed and giants were reduced to appearing in sideshows and sometimes as a gimmicky way to open a shopping plaza. But acting in film and television offered a respectable living. The American giantess Sandy Allen (1955–2008) was seven feet seven inches, a full inch taller than Anna Swan, and Sandy was billed as the World's Tallest Living Woman. Born in Shelbyville, Indiana, she gave a memorable performance as the giantess who rescues Casanova from drowning in the Thames River in Fellini's 1976 movie, *Casanova*.

The most successful show business giant was Detroit-born Richard Kiel (1939–2014). He had a mild case of acromegaly, the hormone disorder that thickens human bones. He became famous as the villain Jaws in the James Bond movies. (The steel contraption he wore over his teeth was so uncomfortable he could keep it in his mouth for only five or ten minutes at a time.)

Kiel was seven feet two inches, and fathered four children with his five-foot-one-inch wife, Diane Rodgers. He also published an autobiography in 2004, with the punning title *Making It Big in the Movies*.

Endings

In the spring of 1979, I began to feel that the co-op wasn't giving me enough privacy to write. I had become its unofficial den mother, and every time I went to the kitchen, I'd run into someone who wanted to chat when I needed to stay in my head and think about my novel on Anna Swan. So I found a single mother with a young daughter to rent my two rooms at the co-op and I finished my novel in a downtown apartment owned by my friend Peggy Gale. It was only a few blocks from Queen Street West, which hadn't been fully gentrified yet, although renovated houses were starting to appear here and there in the Bohemian neighbourhood. I had many new writer friends like Katherine Govier, Margaret Atwood, Erika Ritter, Katherine Ashenburg, literary critic and author Alberto Manguel, who championed my fiction. Suddenly, I was part of the Canadian literary community, working hard like most writers of my generation to create an audience for Canadian books that had been overlooked for American and British bestsellers. Writing in a country with a small population can turn writers into activists in order to protect their literature, and that was the case with many of us.

The ABS Company was disbanded, and I started teaching creative writing. In the future, a university teaching job would be the way to pay my bills. As a professor, I could structure my day into blocks of time, so I wouldn't be interrupted.

A video made in 1985 at 15 Dance Lab in Toronto shows me reading excerpts from my published novel about Anna Swan.

Our faces are smooth and youthful. Margaret Dragu wears quilted white shorts and a matching white top. I'm sitting on top of a ladder, dressed in a white blouse and long flowing white skirt so vast it covers the ladder's bottom rung. The setup is designed to make me look seven feet tall, and there are amusing photographs of me drinking tea from a tiny china teacup designed for a child. *The giantess at home.*

Although my stage work has acquired more polish, Margaret's kinetic genius holds the performance together. A few years later, she and I co-edit *Mothers Talk Back*, a collection of interviews about writers and artists juggling motherhood with their careers.

By then, she's living in Vancouver and Christopher and I have broken up. Differences were starting to appear between us. We respected each other's privacy but I suspected he was sleeping with other women on his business travels, and I felt troubled by his stacks of *Playboy* and *Penthouse*. He kept them by his bed like leftovers, dispensed with and forgotten. One morning, I noticed a cover of his *Hustler* magazine, showing a woman's body being fed into a meat grinder. I felt like a heroine in a horror movie. Why buy a magazine with such a grisly sexist image? When he came into my bedroom he saw a stack of literary magazines, books on feminism by authors like Gloria Steinem and Andrea Dworkin, and academic publications like *Signs*—a journal about women and culture and society. One day he picked up a copy of *Signs* and shook his head. All this stuff about women as a separate subject! Aren't there just people anymore?

I bit my lip.

Our relationship ended when Sam turned eleven. I asked him to move in with me and he rented a big house near Samantha's school with the idea that she could spend more time with us. However, our new living arrangement collapsed when we combined our domestic routines. He made more money than I did and he was used to running things his way. Despite my best intentions, I once again chafed under the traditional expectations of how a wife-like partner should behave. The day we broke up, I dreamed I was leaving behind a Victorian mansion with ten-foot ceilings.

Its walls were covered in giant diamonds that winked and shone on the flocked wallpaper. Their dazzle was almost blinding, but I could make out the figures of Christopher and Samantha's father waving goodbye to me from the mansion's large bay window.

Failure and humiliation

A refrain goes round and round in my head:

You failed again at making a family. What's the matter with you?
You're a bad mother. That's the problem.
Your second relationship has gone up in flames.
Your child doesn't want to live with you.
You don't have enough time for her.
You should never have left your husband.
You don't have enough money.
You're stressed all the time.
You don't live in a good neighbourhood.
You drive an old Ford, a very decrepit red Ford.
Your daughter has to take the subway to school.
You don't earn enough (like him) to put her in private school.
You don't live close to her private school, like her father.
You don't bake Christmas shortbread cookies in
    the shape of stars like her grandmother.
Say it again: You're a bad mother, a bad, bad mother.
    You can't hold a family together. No wonder
    your daughter doesn't want to live with you.
You're a bad, bad, bad, bad, bad, bad, bad, bad mother.

This is how it happens:

The phone rings late one afternoon, just as I'm walking in the door to my apartment. My daughter isn't back from school yet. I assume it's her and my nerves begin to jangle. She has started going to a private girls' school, which is twenty-five minutes away by subway from my Queen Street apartment.

At first, I was against the change of schools, but the teachers in her public school near me were over-extended and her grades were poor. So I'm pleased she likes her new school but I haven't admitted to myself how uneasy I feel about a ten-and-a-half-year-old, even an independent ten-and-a-half-year-old, using the subway. She and I have practised riding it together, and it's the early eighties, and some parents, including myself, think riding the subway teaches self-sufficiency. I always get home before she does. She isn't a latch-key kid. Still, she's a kid. And it's a tiring trip to her school, first on the streetcar and then by subway.

On the phone that afternoon, my mother says brusquely that she needs me to come to her Forest Hill house. She's holding an important family meeting and my daughter is there. Feeling un-settled, I drive up as fast as I can.

In my mother's kitchen, my ex-husband, my mother, and my daughter sit waiting. The faces of the adults are stony. My daughter looks nervous.

We called you here for a reason, my mother announces. Sam's too young to take the subway from your apartment. Her father's house is near her school, so she's going to live full-time with him.

She says it decisively, as if I don't have a voice in their deci-sion. I don't know what shocks me more: that my mother has gone behind my back or that they both think I have to be told what to do because I'm not sensible like them. Surely they know I'm not unreasonable when it comes to my daughter's rights. Okay, maybe they don't.

Her father thinks where I live is scandalous. He says I'm downwardly mobile, fancy words for poor. He doesn't want his daughter growing up in a lower-class neighbourhood of Portuguese immigrants, office workers, and artists.

I ask my daughter if living full-time with her father is what she wants, and she nods eagerly. My heart does a somersault. Of course she wants it. He has set up a bedroom in his coach house just for her. Her best friend lives next door and the school is only a block away. I'd want to live there too if I were her. It's comfortable and convenient and she can stop going to and fro between our houses. But if she moves in with her father, I won't have much time with her.

I think of how I must appear to her: a bone-tired mother, living from paycheque to paycheque in a modest Queen Street apartment, driving a second-hand clunker of a car with outlandish 1950s fins. It looks nothing like the Mercedes and limousines that pick up the other children from her school. No wonder she hides behind the junior school building and waits for her classmates to go home before she comes over to me. My mother and my ex-husband are waiting impatiently. I want to be like the defiant single mother who ridicules her accusers in the country and western hit "Harper Valley PTA." Maybe you know the song? She calls out the hypocrisy of the PTA when its members tell her she's a bad mother because her skirts are too short and she goes out for drinks with men. But I've lost my voice.

My daughter looks embarrassed about them putting me on the spot, although I can tell that she wants to do what they're saying. So, very reluctantly, I say yes, and she murmurs, Oh Mommy. You're so strong.

Am I strong? I feel weak. I feel humiliated. In less than an hour, I've lost my parental right to have her live with me every two weeks. Unless I want to go to court, and I don't want to expose my daughter to a legal fight. They also have a point. Living full-time in his house will make it easier for her to go to her new school and see her friends. I want her comfortable and happy. Why didn't I see this coming? To-ing and fro-ing between our houses no longer works in this new situation. The hard job of daily childcare is over; I won't have the domestic struggles of raising a teenager, which she'll soon be. I'll be like a weekend father, and Sam and I will go away on holidays together.

The meeting breaks up and my daughter goes home with her father. She has her things at his house, so there's no need to come home with me. She'll pick up the rest of her belongings on the weekend. I stand there awkwardly with my mother while my ex throws me a triumphant look as he goes out the door. I leave right afterwards. I can't bear to find out if my mother feels triumphant too.

My mother and I don't talk about what happened. Something occurred that is too terrible to address. She doesn't apologize for going behind my back and I don't apologize for being the bad mother she clearly thinks I am. In the years to come, she will continue to be very generous with the time she spends babysitting. When I become successful, she will make a habit of telling people I was named after her favourite cocker spaniel dog. It was true, and I knew she liked dogs better than people, but her comment implied a warning: don't get a swelled head. And she will never, not once, tell me I have been a good mother to my daughter.

It will take me years before I can put aside my mother's withering judgment of my parenting, and still more years before I can accept my strengths as a mother without hearing her disapproving voice in my ear.

WHEN A MARRIAGE breaks up, no matter which person leaves, there's usually an assumption that the divorce is the woman's fault, that if she had only been more sympathetic, more sexy and alluring, more generous-minded, more intelligent and far-seeing, if she had only asked for less and given more, if she had only done what women do, which is manage the emotional labour of relationships, there would be no separation and the children would have been spared the hardship of divorce. Just as I had been expected to set the tone with sexually aggressive men as a college student, I felt the same expectations operating in my family relationships after my divorce. In many WASP families, including mine, the squeaky wheel is wrong because it squeaks. And although it was never stated directly, the allegation that I had failed to hold my marriage together bobs away in the undertow of my emotional life, along with frequent requests for me to swallow my feelings in order to protect my child, a request I took seriously but, as far as I could tell, was never asked of my ex-husband.

New beginnings

Six months later, on one of our outings, my daughter and I sit chatting at the restaurant at the top of Toronto's CN Tower. She seems happy, and I'm enchanted by her delight in how slowly the tower revolves, revealing with every foot of its relentless pivot views of the leafy neighbourhoods below us where cars can be seen crawling like beetles.

I order drinks: a milkshake for her and a cocktail for myself. It arrives in a tall frosted glass topped with a small turquoise umbrella. I give my daughter the tiny parasol; the waitress smiles at her. My daughter smiles back as she sips her shake.

Outside the glass of the restaurant window, the sun is shining, and it comes to me, in a burst of astonishment, that there are still places like this tourist restaurant where people enjoy themselves with sporty cocktails. It's as if I've come to the end of a long tunnel and landed feet-first back in the world. In ten years, I've lost two major relationships with men I loved, and although by traditional accounts I have failed at what women are supposed to do well, I feel clear-headed and freer of other people's expectations. My daughter says she likes living at her father's house and seeing me on weekends, and I tell her a Toronto university has hired me to teach creative writing. The days of scrambling to make a living are over. It's time to face life on my own, without searching for a man to validate me.

Part Three

THE LAND OF CELEBRITY

IF SOMEONE TOLD me early on that I would be happy living in New York City I would have laughed in disbelief. My first visit there isn't auspicious. I fly to New York in February 1979 with my friend, the writer Katherine Govier, to research Anna Swan's performances during the 1860s at Barnum's American Museum on Broadway.

Katherine and I have rooms at the Royalton Hotel on West Forty-Fourth Street. It's a glamorous boutique hotel now but it was a dive when we stayed in it—grimy, poorly lit, and uncomfortable. We heard rumours that bedbugs were a possibility. They are always a possibility in New York hotels, posh or poor. So are cockroaches. We hear them scrambling behind the walls of our bedroom, which looks out onto the brick wall of the next building.

Our change purses are falling apart from being opened and shut so many times to pay for items such as bottled water and sandwiches that are cheaper at home. The city feels like it's obliterating our identities, turning Katherine and me into hicks without bothering to find out what kind of hicks we are. We're Canadian hicks—that much is obvious. We don't say *caw-fee* for coffee or talk about walking in the *pak*. We don't call pizza *pie* and chocolate *chaw-clet*, and because we don't know any better, we make the mistake of asking the taxi to take us to Forty-Fourth Street West instead of the way it's usually said, West Forty-Fourth Street.

But the research is going well. Better than I expected. The building that houses Barnum's American Museum is no longer there, but I can find where it stood on Broadway and Greene Street, just as I find the street address of Barnum's favourite restaurant, Delmonico's, where he sometimes took his "prodigies," as he called the giants and dwarfs who exhibited with him at his American Museum.

The Anglican church where Anna went to pray is still on Broadway opposite the west wall of Wall Street. Trinity Church is a graceful revolutionary building with a spire like a ladyfinger cookie, and when I visit, taking a seat near its altar, images come rushing in of Anna's huge body doubled over in prayer, her enormous skirts flowing in three directions at once, threatening to smother whoever sits near her in cascading waves of taffeta and crinoline, her large hands clasped delicately across the ruffles of her blouse, hand-sewn by a New York seamstress and tailored to her size.

I sit in the pew and close my eyes, imagining the enormous amount of space she would take up. With a sweep of her stiff Victorian petticoats, she could knock someone like me off their seat and onto the church floor—*Make room, make room*, her body seems to be proclaiming. *I'm big so please move over!*

I'm channelling Anna the way novelists do with their characters, imagining I'm inside her giant body, thinking her thoughts. Her story, like mine, is a story of not fitting, and for years, she represented my worst fears about my femininity, the nightmare possibility that I might become a giantess too, and now I'm here in her old stomping grounds, wanting, without fear or judgment, to understand how the world looked to her, how it felt being Anna Swan. Is it me, or Anna who is standing on Broadway staring in shock at the out-of-tune band tootling outside Barnum's American Museum? Is it me, or her who sees the old-guard New Yorkers strolling by, shaking their heads in disgust and burying their noses behind white handkerchiefs to demonstrate their disdain for Barnum's show palace? They're wearing black clothes like the good Puritans they are, and they're horrified by the way their city is changing into a metropolis they don't recognize. Changing, in their eyes, into a fleshpot of sin where citizens lack all sense of decorum. Anna won't know—but I do—that Barnum, with his love of entertainment and the way he invites his audiences to solve hoaxes like the Fiji mermaid, will show his fellow Americans how to kick off the last traces of their Puritanism and have a good time.

I'M THIRTY-FOUR THAT afternoon in New York in 1979. Anna was sixteen when she came here in 1862 to work for Barnum. She would have been used to drawing attention, thanks to the fall fairs back home where her family exhibited her as the Infant Giantess. There would have been farmers who called out rude comments and children who giggled and pointed.

Not all of the gawking would've been mean or derisory. Some, if not a great deal of the attention, would have been expressed as gazes of wonder and astonishment, and there must have been glances of admiration. Many people might very well have looked at her the way we look at a magnificent mountain. After all, if you're tall, you must be acknowledged and dealt with, like a celebrity of the body. Maybe it's no accident that many world leaders are tall; they are, by virtue of their size, already somebody to reckon with. So Anna may have enjoyed and even needed the gapes and stares and then felt secretly ashamed of herself, like the embarrassment many of us feel when we overshare on Facebook.

She lived at the American Museum, which Barnum owned before he went into the circus business. He billed it as a place of learning because he had re-created the British idea of a museum as a mass entertainment show palace, the first of its kind in North America.

The place was nothing less than a dressed-up carny barker show, even though Barnum advertised the giants and dwarfs as if they were serious lecturers who would tell you, the unenlightened audience member, how to deduce the normal from the abnormal, and you would go away edified that you had learned something about yourself that you didn't know before.

Or so his bogus advertising claimed.

When she arrived, Anna had no idea what a future with Barnum would bring. At the museum, she will be paid $1,000 a month to give talks to New York audiences on the way her size affected her life. In her lectures, she will describe having her clothes specially made, and sometimes she wraps a tape measure around her waist and gives it to a woman in the audience to wrap around hers, knowing it will go three times around the waist of the average woman. Anna will also act in spoofs of Shakespearean plays. In one of her performances, she plays Lady Macbeth while Commodore Nutt, the dwarf who plays Macbeth, speaks his lines sitting on her shoulder. Their act is intended to be an amusing burlesque, but it mocks her failure to live up to the Victorian notion of the ideal woman, who was petite and ladylike and would never dream of taking up more space than a man.

How did she manage in New York after growing up in the backwoods of Nova Scotia? When I think of her entering such a large, vibrant place for the first time, feeling frightened and uncertain, I bristle at the thought of her being disdained by the nineteenth-century New Yorkers who strode by Barnum's showplace with their noses in the air.

What was she doing there, she must have wondered. Or, more to the point, what am I doing in New York? Everything about the city strikes me as nonsensical. I'm amazed at the foolishness of the joggers in Central Park trying so hard to be healthy while inhaling draughts of the smoggy city air with its undeniable carcinogens. And I'm irritated by the overcrowded streets and pedestrians who walk straight at you without stepping out of the way, jostling each other and talking in a loud, shouting manner. Their behaviour triggers the aggressive side of my personality—a side well hidden beneath my polite Canadian exterior. When they bump into me without apologizing, I begin to push people back and they stare at me in surprise. I imagine how satisfying it would feel to hit one of them over their head with my umbrella. It's raining, the air stinks of car fumes and industrial pollution, and I want to go home.

Katherine hurries me off to tea at the Algonquin Hotel, where Canadians who feel homesick for Canada go, and inside its subdued, wood-panelled rooms I calm down.

I put my first response to New York City in a passage from my novel about Anna Swan meeting P.T. Barnum for the first time. In my story, he invites her to dinner at Delmonico's and asks her to sit on top of a table he has rigged up like a throne so she can entertain the mudsills, as New Yorkers used to be called. (In Victorian times, it was said New Yorkers had river mud on their window-sills.) I describe Anna's amazement at the setup. Instead of sitting on the floor, as she did in Nova Scotia, so her head would be level with the heads of her siblings sitting in chairs at the table, she's rigged up like a queen on a dais that rises above the heads of the other diners. In the novel, she delights her new employer with an entertaining lecture on the Canadian cough drop, exclaiming: "It was easy to see from where I sat, staring down at diners' faces staring up at me, their cheeks bulging with Timbales a la française, that Americans were the world's strangest people."

Myth-struck in a fabled space

Seven years later I'm back in New York. I'm no longer a novelist channelling the life and times of a Victorian giantess but a fellow traveller looking for a home that fits. My search feels mythic, so I can't help talking in metaphors now to explain why I feel so restless at this point in my life. Without admitting it to myself, I've started searching the world for the place I belong, and I can no more explain what I'm doing than a bird can describe why they fly south. Instinct and need drive me.

In *Gulliver's Travels*, Gulliver meets people who are sixty feet tall, but the gigantic land they inhabit matches their shocking size. *Where is my Brobdingnagian world*, I often wonder. In Brobdingnag, even the rats are big, standing as tall and stiff as mastiff dogs with tails two yards long, while mastiffs are equal in bulk to four elephants. Of course, it wasn't so much a physical reflection of my size that I was seeking but a place where I felt my ambitions as a writer, along with the way I moved in the world, would be understood by the people around me.

Or would my quest for that place be a failure? Although she searched for home in many places, including England and the United States, Anna Swan never found a place that accepted her as a person. Her parochial birthplace in Nova Scotia couldn't accommodate her extraordinary size, and her life as a giantess in New York City was exhausting and exploitative, although Barnum paid her a good salary at his New York museum. In London, England, she and her husband were colonial oddities. Seville, Ohio, was Anna's last stop, but the small-town folk in Buckeye country where she and her husband raised Shorthorn cattle saw the two giants as rich show business people and viewed them with suspicion.

Anna's giant farmhouse didn't help. The house had seventeen rooms, fourteen-foot ceilings, and eight-and-a-half-foot doors. The furniture was made to order and the historian Phyllis Blakeley said in her account of Anna Swan's life that visitors had to climb up the rungs of a chair to sit on it.

In 1978, when I had travelled to Seville to research her last years, I discovered their house had been torn down in 1947 because the giant farmhouse was too expensive to heat. The Ohio people I interviewed were proud she had lived in Seville, but like many people in North American communities they hadn't valued their history enough to preserve her home as a heritage site.

Anna died in her sleep of heart failure at the age of forty-two. Her tomb sits in Seville's Mound Hill Cemetery, where she lies next to her husband, who insisted on being buried beside her even though he remarried after her death. A giant stone woman towers above Anna's grave, bearing the words: *I will behold thy face with righteousness. I should be satisfied when I wake, with thy likeness.*

The inscription is from Psalm 17, verse 15, and it suggests she had doubts about her own appearance.

ON MY SECOND journey to New York City, it helps in my search for a home that I have fallen in love with a kind-hearted Jewish man from Brooklyn who, like me, was holidaying at a yoga camp in the Bahamas. Joe is two decades older, and something about the shape of his chin and his ears reminds me of my father, although my new boyfriend isn't a workaholic doctor. He's a former NASA engineer who works as an employment counsellor at New York's City Hall, and he puts more time into his family and friends than his job.

I'm impressed with his laid-back lifestyle and he's impressed that I'm a writer whose novel about Anna Swan, *The Biggest Modern Woman of the World*, has been successfully published in Canada, the United Kingdom, and the United States.

It also helps that I've negotiated an unusual tenured position at York University in Toronto where I teach one year on and one year off, provided I don't receive a salary for the year I take off. My job means I can visit Joe when I'm not teaching, and although our relationship won't last, it's the start of me living off and on in New York City for the next six years.

The first night in bed in his apartment in Sheepshead Bay, I dream I'm tumbling head over heels, flying like Henry Hudson's ghost ship across the Catskill Mountains and the broad flat tongue of the Hudson with its shimmery river light, landing feet first in a mythic world called America.

My radiant dream, with its sense of wonder and fear, leaves me breathless. It's the late eighties, before Donald Trump has hijacked the world of American politics, and in my dream, America is still capable of offering a welcoming vision of itself to the traveller, inviting you in to enjoy its grand pageantry, its endless vista of freedom and possibility that suggest here there might be enough room to breathe.

I wake up myth-struck. I've somersaulted into a vast fabled space where social myths leap and spin. America doesn't move slowly forward or backward in increments like my homeland but progresses through ferocious debates over cultural values that are enacted on the stage of public life. One isn't made American by living there; one becomes a citizen of the land by arguing with other citizens about what it means to be American.

I've read Alexis de Tocqueville's book *Democracy in America*, and his statements about the pleasure Americans take in political discussions and harangues come back to me. A French historian and thinker, de Tocqueville said American debating clubs were a substitute for theatrical entertainments and were so lively and interesting that housewives attended as a way to relax after doing domestic chores. An American speaks to you as if he is addressing a meeting, de Tocqueville noted.

America in the late eighties wasn't much different from the days when de Tocqueville wrote about it in 1837. It still isn't. The digital sea change, which has transformed the world, hasn't changed how America presents itself; it's only amplified and intensified the way the country's political dramas are publicized and enacted.

I've come to New York before the triumph of digital technology, before Instagram and Facebook, and the political conflicts that are unrolling before me—as dramatic as the sweep of the Hudson River at the entrance to Manhattan—are played out on the ubiquitous twenty-foot television screens above many New York City bars, or on the huge television sets in homes and apartments. America is a theatrical culture and its epic battles give the life of each American a mythological tinge.

As a witness to the dramatic panorama of the country's political landscape, I'm learning that each American citizen plays a role in the mythmaking that goes on in America, and nobody does that more clearly than American celebrities, who act out their parts like characters in a morality play. I think of Miss Muckle, my high school English teacher with the Dickensian name, who taught us the work of the nineteenth-century English playwright George Bernard Shaw. She drilled it into our heads that each one of Shaw's characters represented an idea, and the conflict between these ideas provided the drama. I can still see her self-satisfied smile when she tells us, her unruly pupils, how Caesar in Shaw's play *Caesar and Cleopatra* represents mercy while Cleopatra represents vengeance, and that Caesar's clemency wins the day.

What would Miss Muckle say about a country where Shavian notions of theatre are literally played out in the daily life of its citizens? Perhaps she wouldn't approve of me applying Shaw's theory of drama to America. Nevertheless, American celebrities are often associated with a contested idea, which they battle over with institutions or other well-known personalities, including politicians, that represent an opposing idea. The celebrities are cheered or shouted down by the public and praised or attacked in the media until one appears to win, and then journalists and news anchors will analyze and reflect on whether this outcome is good for their country.

Self-reflection isn't the way America usually performs itself, but of course, it's there too. Essentialism, as a method for understanding people from another culture, is only useful to a point.

Celebrity scandals play a large role in America's public dramas. In the 1980s, the pious televangelists Jim Bakker and Jimmy Swaggart were exposed as cheats and hypocrites, with Swaggart caught up in two prostitution scandals and Bakker going to jail for defrauding his congregation (although Bakker's jail sentence was later reduced to five years, so the degree to which honesty and justice won out over vice isn't obvious in his case). When I lived in New York, the Bill Clinton and Monica Lewinsky scandal and O.J. Simpson's murder trial in the late nineties were just around the corner in time.

As anyone who watches the news understands, some American values, like freedom and human rights vis-à-vis the cruel legacy of slavery, are performed again and again like a depressing downer loop in a Wagnerian ring cycle. Espousing a credo of racism and conspiracy theories, Donald Trump, the forty-fifth president, wriggled into power like a reincarnation of Lizard Man only to be challenged by Captain America, played by Joe Biden. But I'm getting ahead of myself.

In New York, I'm discovering that Americans excel at mythologizing themselves. For many New Yorkers, life in their city is enough. Who needs actual success when you can walk around inside a fantasy bubble of your personal hopes and ambitions, performing your future for everyone to see?

Colin, a New York friend, is using a video camera he built to film a commercial that features the tickertape parade of Gulf War troops marching up Broadway. It's June 1991, and in his television ad, a huge vacuum cleaner sucks up the detritus left behind on the red carpet winding through the city. Colin tells me he's ashamed to be making a commercial that exploits the deaths of thousands of civilians and soldiers in a useless and unnecessary war. Looking resigned, he shakes his head and mutters that mythmaking takes precedence over truth.

One evening in the Village, a waitress breaks into an aria from an opera while she serves customers at a restaurant. The waitress confides that she is going to be a famous opera singer like Maria Callas and then she belts out a song from *Carmen*. My friends and I clap and laugh while the people at the nearby tables shrug and get on with their meals.

A few days later, walking past a restaurant near Washington Square, I pass four chefs standing in the window chopping vegetables with meat knives the size of sabers.

When the chefs look up and see me, one of them lifts his hand above his head to acknowledge my size, and then the four of them raise their huge knives in a salute. I smile and wave. Wholehearted approval like this doesn't happen at home, where I sometimes feel like I might break the furniture if I'm not careful how I sit on it.

Canada has begun to feel like a go-along box. One of my novels, *The Last of the Golden Girls*, draws two complaints of obscenity after I read an excerpt on a Canadian radio station. The novel describes summers in Ontario's cottage country when young women compete for boyfriends and, later, husbands. Following a six-month investigation, the complaints are dropped after a detective in the Edmonton morality squad deems the excerpt "charming." A few years later, a Canadian customs official confiscates my novel *The Wives of Bath* from the knapsack of a University of Waterloo professor on the grounds that it's obscene.

It's embarrassing to live in a country where customs officials confuse literature with pornography.

Perhaps America will have more room.

New York and the ambition box

There's no doubt about it: New York is an ambition box. It's where many people go to be successful in their work. Or let me put it another way: New York is a city with thousands of little boxes in which you can aspire to and dream of a new, more potent public self, a bigger self that isn't self-conscious about taking up space, a self that feels it has every right to take up as much space as it needs. These small incubating units of self-worth are the city's neighbourhoods, and each neighbourhood block is its own world, a box in itself. In the eighties, when I'm there, you can find everything you could possibly want in each New York block. Like bumping by accident into editors such as Karen Durbin, who works for the *Village Voice*, gives me journalism assignments, and becomes a friend. Like having your eyelids tattooed so you no longer need eyeliner, or your jeans mended and cleaned in an hour at the dry cleaner shop, which is right next door to the office offering tuina

massage, and, if you're up for more adventures, the late-night sex
and bondage club and, not to forget, the basement hidey-hole of
the street-corner psychic, because fortune-telling is popular in the
allegedly rational world of Manhattan.

When I live in New York, the city's population hovers just
above eighteen million, and its air pollution is arguably worse
than it is now. The longer I stay in the city the paler my complexion becomes, until my skin has the pallor of a root vegetable. But
I'm drawn by the lure of America and the possibilities it offers for
a prosperous writing career. *We are all Americans now, even when
we live someplace else,* I gush in a piece of flash fiction. I feel myself
more at home in New York than I ever have elsewhere.

In the spring of 1989, as gently as I can, I break up with Joe.
I've become uncomfortable with his Republican politics, and
the way he admires Ronald Reagan for cutting welfare costs. The
twenty-year difference in our ages worries me too. We're eating
lunch in his one-bedroom apartment in Sheepshead Bay. It over-
looks a busy handball court and the Atlantic Ocean is just a few
blocks away, with his yacht club and nearby boardwalk and Russian restaurants where we sometimes go for a meal. And just over
thirty-seven minutes away on his motorcycle, rising like a mirage
above the Norway maples and white mulberry trees in his Brooklyn neighbourhood, are the towers of Manhattan. He's fond of
saying the city is our toy land where we go to play.

This afternoon, he interrupts me as I'm struggling to tell him
why I want to see other people, and says in his loveable "toidy-toid"
Brooklyn accent: You need to think what you're doing, kid. Men
don't look at forty-year-old women.

I'm forty-three and he's just made a huge mistake in saying this, since I'm the kind of person who objects to being told I can't do something. Just to spite you, I'll charge ahead and do it. Warnings like Joe's don't frighten me—they provoke defiance. I'll show you, I vow, and away I go—sometimes without checking if defeating the challenge is really how I want to spend my time.

In this case, it decidedly is, because slowly, ever so slowly, Aphrodite Mode is starting to dominate my life. I was using the term in the eighties, a decade when the internet hadn't monetized so much of our lives. In fact, Aphrodite Mode is now a fashion brand on Instagram that sells women's clothing and apparel. But for me, Aphrodite Mode was a way of being that gave pleasure the same value as work—starting with my morning Americano and one or two fluffy Manhattan corn muffins. Poof! So much for the tyranny of my father's Protestant ethos of work until you drop.

A bestselling book—*Goddesses in Everywoman* by Jean Shinoda Bolen, an American psychiatrist and Jungian analyst—supports my new approach. Published in 1984, Bolen's non-fiction book told women to tap into the powerful archetypal forces of the Greek goddesses that exist within them and influence what they feel and what they do.

According to Bolen, Aphrodite isn't hurt by her relationships because she doesn't let them define her like Persephone and some of the other goddesses do. Basking in the glow of her attention, we feel more interesting and attractive because Aphrodite affirms us instead of subjecting us to criticism. Joe, with his attentiveness and his ability to enjoy life, shared many of Aphrodite's qualities, and I treated what I learned from him as the gift it was.

Like a traveller who starts exploring a block or two in a new neighbourhood, and then gradually expands her investigation into ever-widening circles, I visit Joe less, and begin renting apartments off and on in Manhattan. When I'm not teaching in Toronto, I spend long stretches of time in New York. It's the place to be if you're a fiction writer in the early nineties. The scene is big enough to include a downtown community of writers in the Village, and a well-to-do group of writers who live in upscale apartments on the Upper East Side.

The first apartment I rent is a grubby, closet-sized affair typical then of the East Village. No doorman, sloppily grouted tiles on the walls of the small lobby, and living quarters so thick with dust I may as well be living in an archaeological tomb. At night, I carefully brush a fresh layer of grime off my bed before I go to sleep. In the day, I'm out and about, writing in coffee shops and dreading the time when I have to return home.

Better apartments follow. A large one-bedroom on Thirteenth Street in the West Village with a doorman and a king-sized bed so vast that I can lose track of a boyfriend who stays over. Later there will be a more commodious corner apartment on Fourteenth Street, owned by an artist who comes to New York to paint.

One morning, in the heavily windowed sunlit space of my Chelsea apartment, I wake up and realize I've become a New Yorker.

Size and the writer

It seems physical size has a metaphysical dimension, because it can't be charted the way you measure someone's height in inches and feet. Its influence is pervasive. It affects how the world looks at you and that, in turn, affects how you look at the world, although I'm not able to tell you exactly how my size alters my vision of what I see around me except to say that my height offers me the perspective of an outsider. Disadvantage is often an advantage for a writer since the perspective it brings helps you notice things that are invisible to other people.

Because it sets you apart, the otherness of extreme height also breeds a feeling of isolation. The critic Alberto Manguel once wrote that my fictional characters exist in a world apart from regular life. It was an observation, not a criticism, and he didn't attribute this characteristic to my height, although there's likely a connection.

MY SECOND NOVEL, *The Last of the Golden Girls*, has just been published in the United States by Jeannette and Dick Seaver, the editors of Arcade Publishing. The couple brought the work of foreign writers like Samuel Beckett and Jean Genet to America, and were instrumental in court battles where they helped end the American censorship of books by Henry Miller and D.H. Lawrence. In those days, the Seavers were famous for being sophisticated literary tastemakers along with other New York editors like Dan Halpern who ran Ecco Press, the small publishing firm that brought out my Anna Swan novel.

For all these reasons, I feel lucky to be with Arcade, and eager to help with publicity for my book.

But when Irene Skolnick, an agent with Curtis Brown, tells me that Gordon Lish wants to talk to me about my second novel at his Random House office, I immediately feel apprehensive. She has unnerved me by hinting that he's prone to sleeping with attractive women writers. Maybe he'll take me under his wing, she says with a wink. Adding to my nervousness, Irene claims that she knows a number of women writers who are grateful for his encouragement and attention.

Does she expect me to play along too? My anxiety is growing by the time I take the elevator up to his office in the Random House building. What should I do if he comes on to me? Should I beat him up? Nope. When I open his door and walk in, it's him, not me, who seems awkward. He stumbles to his feet, looking flustered, and I realize he didn't expect me to be so tall. Whistling between his teeth, he says something like, You're a big woman. I think, but don't say, And you're a short man. I'm too nervous to joke. Besides, he's a compelling figure with his shiny silver hair and piercing eyes. The skin of his handsome face glows the same patrician shade of tan as his safari suit.

Recovering from the surprise of my height, Gordon Lish suavely pulls himself together. He tells me in his friendly, paternal voice that *The Last of the Golden Girls* is very clever and off we go to lunch.

I'm relieved and impressed by his gentlemanly manners. He never puts the moves on me, and the generous way he dedicates himself to helping other writers is impressive. He specializes in helping them carve out the deadwood from their prose so the power of their words stands out. His minimalist technique made the short stories of Raymond Carver famous, and he uses it himself in his own novels.

Soon he's introducing me to the students who take his popular writing workshops. I meet writers like Ben Marcus, Christine Schutt, Amy Hempel, Dawn Raffel, William Tester, and Mark Richard, who had just won the 1990 PEN/Hemingway Award for his story collection *The Ice at the Bottom of the World*.

They tell me Gordon is a demanding teacher who asks them to read their stories out loud. As soon as he's bored, he makes the writer retrace their steps back to the last provocative sentence and start again from that point.

He believes writers should place themselves in jeopardy with their work. He has no interest in anyone who wants to keep their fiction safe from embarrassing or humiliating revelations.

Through Gordon, I get to know Diane Williams, who writes original short fiction (or flash fiction, as these stories are sometimes called). She's new to New York too, and she convinces me to leave Irene Skolnick and accept a contract with her agent, Kim Witherspoon, who is young and looking for clients.

One afternoon, Diane and I attend a reading by Gordon at a downtown Barnes & Noble bookstore. He sits behind the author's table, signing books and dressed, as always, in a beige safari suit. I know him well enough by now to be aware that he suffers from a bad case of psoriasis and that he uses a sunbed tan to cover it up. A lineup of middle-aged New York women wait, clutching close to their chest copies of his books.

One of his books, his novel *Zimzum*, contains a section about all the women his male narrator wants to have sex with while his wife is dying of cancer. At a reading a few years later in the Ontario countryside, Gordon will maintain his composure while he's clapped off the stage by the audience, who want to stop him reading that same passage. Talk about writing fiction that puts you in jeopardy! Gordon's own wife is dying of cancer, and the implication is that he is the male character. No one can accuse Gordon of not following his own advice.

Zimzum has provoked disdain and outrage from reviewers, but the women in the bookshop don't seem to mind. They stand whispering and giggling with each other, throwing admiring glances his way. Gordon is embarrassed by the fuss they are making over him, and he whispers that he finds it weird to be the object of his fans' devotion. It's very sad they need it so much, he adds, nodding in their direction. He's at his best helping other writers find their voice, and although he has found his, he doesn't seem to care how many readers buy his books. It's the experimental aspect in fiction that interests him, the solitary pushing of literary boundaries that allows him to revel in word play and, ultimately, examine himself by using language in a way that's certain to shock or offend.

That afternoon, I can't help wondering if shyness is the reason for his contempt of popular success. Or maybe he doesn't care because he has the respect and friendship of critics like Harold Bloom along with the devotion of his students and his modest share of readers.

As I will find out over the next few years, he's a self-styled buccaneer determined to make the publishing industry pay him the ransom he seeks—a highbrow reputation for his literary experiments and the right to publish writers whose work he likes. His love of short, chiselled sentences and his clothes likely owes something to Hemingway, who was often photographed wearing a safari suit. You better sit up and take notice, Lish is saying with his outfits and his prose, OR ELSE.

Gordon's pen name is Captain Fiction, a pseudonym that lets

you know he intends to be the architect of his own myth. There is a lot of personal myth-making going around when I'm in New York. The book pages are dominated by the rock star male novelists who have emerged as cult literary figures despite the critics in the 1970s who worried women writers were taking over literature. So much for feminist authors upending the careers of male writers.

The group includes English writers like Martin Amis, Kazuo Ishiguro, and Julian Barnes and American male novelists like Norman Mailer, Bret Easton Ellis, and Jay McInerney. Like some of these writers, Gordon is known for outrageous behaviour, and he has been heard to shout to young women editors as he enters a party: Where's the fucking room, girl? A remark like that would get him quickly hustled to Human Resources now.

Most of the male writers I'm meeting display some version of bad-boy antics. An ambitious young man in my circle of writer friends carries around his novel in a small leatherette suitcase that resembles a doctor's bag and brags non-stop about the day when he'll be as well-known as Hemingway. No one tries to talk him out of his fantasy. He's too vulnerable and boyish in his cowboy clothes and styled hair.

Another young man I come across is drinking martinis at a Manhattan bar dressed in an old-fashioned three-piece business suit. A gold watch dangles from the fob in his vest and a pair of tortoise-shell glasses perch on his nose as he sits on his stool, noisily turning the pages of a thick manuscript while surreptitiously glancing around the bar to see the effect he is having. I don't know him; my companion doesn't know him either, but it's clear he wants attention because he looks for all the world like he has stepped out of the pages of the *New Yorker* magazine, circa

1946. Is he playing the part of the famous Thomas Wolfe, the writer from North Carolina, or Wolfe's famous editor Maxwell Perkins? Perhaps he isn't sure himself.

Then there are the monologues of the late Spalding Gray, who was well-known for his droll performances, especially *Monster in a Box*, his show about the two-thousand-page-novel he was writing before he drowned himself in the Hudson River.

When you saw *Monster in a Box*, you knew Spalding was never going to finish his novel, and that was the point. He wasn't selling his literature—he was selling himself as a showman.

One way or another, these attention-seekers are hoping to find their public by doing what my mother's relatives, who came from solid Presbyterian stock, used to call making "a show of yourself."

When I get together with other New York women writers, we joke about creating mythic identities to sell our books, and the name of my friend the late Kathy Acker comes up. Although she was once part of Toronto's conceptual art scene, I didn't meet her then; I met her later in Toronto at a reading with William Burroughs where the audience loved her edgy punk presentation, the heavily tattooed muscled arms, the sassy New Yorker drawl, and the raw, in-your-face fiction that mixed literary storytelling techniques with film and performance art. She had constructed a ferocious public persona, but in person she was kind and compassionate and I happened to know she still slept with her childhood teddy bear. She was the only woman writer in my experience who performed herself in the same style as many of the rock star male novelists, and all of these celebrated writers were helping to ease the way towards the contemporary trend of sharing mythic identities on social media platforms.

A few years after I met him, Gordon was fired from Knopf because the books he acquired didn't sell enough copies. Publishing in America has become a corporate business, and Gordon was one of the first victims of the belief that every single book is expected to pay for itself, and only (or mostly only) the bottom line matters. Editors are no longer able to rely on commercial bestsellers to pay for the experimental work of authors like Gordon that are written to challenge reader expectations, and his artistic mission seems like a cautionary tale about the dangers in America of ignoring your audience.

To quote de Tocqueville again, democratic nations like the United States will habitually prefer the useful to the beautiful, and they will require the beautiful to be useful.

And yet, isn't there a way to forge a literary career without concentrating on writing bestsellers, I would ask myself. To write for yourself and your friends as Virginia Woolf and her husband, Leonard, did during the days of the Bloomsbury group? The answer is that of course it's possible, but your books won't be respected unless they reach a wide audience, and Lish's storied reputation came primarily from editing the work of Raymond Carver, whose books of short fiction did sell in large numbers.

New York writers like my friend Diane Williams have handled the dilemma by having their books of fiction published by a non-profit publisher, Dalkey Archive Press. Diane's literary reputation has only grown, although publishing with non-profits is a quieter path and not one that many American writers tend to choose.

SO WHAT AM I really learning living in New York in the early nineties about dealing with my height, my writing, and being myself? I had already discovered how to exploit personal obsessions in Toronto's performance community, and before that, the use of my height in eye-catching photographs in newspaper tabloids. And before that, there was the college boy who taught me how to dramatize my height in the Umbrella Dance. But never before have I seen so many people so enthusiastically performing who they are. Why did it take me so long to get it? My size is a bonus, not a drawback. It's part of who I am, and the mythic spell cast by height, plus the power of words, sets me apart as a writer. Make use of everything that's yours, in other words, because it's unique to you.

After all, what matters here is chutzpah, so drop any leftover Presbyterian notions you might still harbour. It's America, the land of celebrity. It's New York, where self-promotion is the natural order of things. It gets you acclaim, and who dares speak against that? Over and over again, I seem to be stumbling across the same lesson that the giantess Anna Swan learned from Barnum: get out there and make a show of yourself. Which is what she did, until, that is, she lived through the horror of two fires at his museum (likely set to collect insurance money), and in order to escape the first fire, she had to be lowered by a derrick handled by eighteen men from a third-storey window—an experience so traumatic it may have led her to leave New York.

Thankfully, no one tried to lower me from a building with a derrick, although I might have found it an interesting experience to write about if they had. My options as a performer were wide open compared to what life offered Anna, and my time in New York City was one of the happiest periods of my life.

Aphrodite mode

1.

Right before the literary whirlwind of New York in the nineties, in the summer of 1989, I come back from a holiday in Greece, pack up my things from my latest New York apartment, and fly to the small airport in Middlebury, Vermont, heading for the Bread Loaf Writers' Conference. I'm dressed in white pants and a white halter top that sets off my Mediterranean tan, a good-time Charlotte assessing new situations for the opportunity to have fun.

I'm eager to experience the ritual of Bread Loaf, an annual series of writing workshops founded in 1926 at Middlebury College. It has a history of famous writers who go there to critique the work of young writers and party in the rustic cottages on the grounds near the Bread Loaf Inn. Its alumni include famous authors like Carson McCullers, Robert Frost, Toni Morrison, Anne Sexton, and John Irving, who recommended me for the conference.

On my first day at Bread Loaf, I notice Bobby, a handsome Black American writer standing by his motorcycle wearing a worn-looking leather jacket and proudly holding up a copy of a book while young women, both Black and white, cluster around him, taking his photograph. It's a fascinating scene, both for the beauty of the man and the landscape and because of the large group of admiring women. In the background soared sixty-foot white pines, the tall straight trees that were used for the masts of Yankee sailing ships.

He is tall, taller than me, with short, curly hair, and a hooded, burning gaze, and when he catches my eye over the heads of his fans, I feel an immediate attraction, but I turn away, embarrassed to be caught staring at a man. Afterwards, I make a point of ignoring him. In the morning, a young woman with frizzy auburn hair brings him a plate of scrambled eggs while the rest of us line up to get our breakfast from the buffet. She is one of his fans. *If that's the kind of service he expects, forget it,* I think.

Every afternoon, after the writing workshops are over, he plays tennis with some of his female followers while the others watch, sitting on the grass by the court, laughing and clapping wildly for Bobby, who always plays against two opponents. It gets me moving, he says with one of his friendly smiles.

And every day, I walk by these tennis matches without so much as a glance, until one evening, he approaches me in the cottage where students and faculty go to drink and asks why I've been ignoring him. I say I hadn't meant to be rude. Pleased, he invites me to play tennis the next day and I accept.

I learned how to play at boarding school and I'm good at the game. But I'm no match for him. He learned to play watching television, he says. Knowing his determination to excel, it's likely true. He prides himself on his cultivated tastes; he drives high-priced motorcycles and goes fly-fishing in places like Scotland and New Brunswick. His great-great-great-grandfather had been a slave in Virginia who knew how to read and write, unlike the white man who owned him. When his literate ancestor was freed in 1832, he started a stagecoach line in Tennessee, where he amassed wealth and acres of land for his children. Bobby, his descendant, comes from a stable middle-class family in St. Louis, Missouri, and he went to an all-white boys' Catholic school there before graduating from Stanford University. He's fond of talking about the lack of discrimination he experienced at his American boys' school, although that's hard to believe.

By the time we meet, he has already published a well-received book of non-fiction about travelling in Africa as a Black American. It's the same book he was holding while the women took his photograph under the pine tree.

In any case, his tennis is very, very good, and soon he and I are playing every afternoon while his group of followers sit on the grass and cheer us on. By the time the two-week workshop is ending, he and I are eating our lunches together and I'm going for rides on his massive Kawasaki bike, my arms wrapped around his waist.

At the closing dance, some of his followers pin a white carnation on his jacket and then dance around him in a frenzy resembling a funky, impromptu fertility rite. I dance over, snatch the flower off his lapel, and eat it while the other women shriek with glee. They appear to see me as their delegate—the woman lucky enough to receive the blessing of this captivating man's attention and love.

2.

I'm single when Bobby and I meet, and I've started to travel to England and to Greece during the summers when I'm not teaching in Toronto or renting an apartment in New York. I'm living inside a narrative of my own making, like the experiences of my two friends that I wrote about in our diaries. However, this time I'm consciously directing what I want to happen and not worrying much when the arc of a romantic encounter makes its inevitable leap from excitement to boredom or disappointment. By the time I go to the Bread Loaf conference I've discovered that most of the men I'm seeing project onto me views of women that are usually based on experiences with their mothers. I ignore their projections. Some of them don't take the time to understand who I am. And even if they are observant, many of them tend to carry around outdated notions of women.

My freewheeling attitude startles people who know me. Some deplore the change while others, like my Toronto editor, beg to hear my stories.

Before the start of the Bread Loaf summer, I have three boyfriends with the same first name and none of the three know about each other. I didn't find three boyfriends with the same name intentionally, but the similarity in their names makes life easier. Hello, Jim? I ask as I pick up the phone, with an inquisitive Valley girl uplift on the last syllable. And of course, he says yes.

You have the attention span of a hummingbird, a female friend says. When another friend hears about the posse of boyfriends, she suggests there's safety in numbers, and her remark feels closer to the truth. I don't want to get hurt again.

Middle-aged women sniff disbelievingly when I tell them how easy it is to meet attractive men.

The men I meet in Aphrodite Mode each have their own appealing qualities, enough to leave me charmed and distracted while I carry on with my writing. What is my appeal? I'm the most overweight I've been and I don't care. A boyfriend tells me that I exude a sense of adventure and he wants to go along on the ride. I'm the happiest I've been in my life because I'm making good money and living a life where I am not affected by other people's judgments. Women are told so many don'ts that it's exhilarating to make up my own rules. I share the generous democratic approach of womanizers like Italian adventurer Giacomo Casanova (1725–1798). As Casanova said once, "I have never made love to a woman whose language I didn't speak because I like to enjoy myself in all my senses at once."

He was fluent in six languages. I speak two, and only one well.

To work, Aphrodite Mode depends on giving myself enough time to relax and look after my body so I feel recharged, and when I take the time to do that I can feel the rush of sexual energy radiating out from me like a force field. The rush is an enthralling sensation, as if I'm about to cast a kinetic web over my surroundings containing the power of pure vitality and the joy of being alive.

However, the following pages aren't going to be filled with explicit accounts of my sexual experiences. I'll leave to your imagination the accounts of intimate moments with my lovers, for their sake and my own, because discretion is part of my code of rules for my single life, along with no married men, no promises, and no ghosting. As a subject, sex has no point except the experience of pleasure. Unless, of course, the experience comes with the subtext of conflict and a revelation of a character's motivations—all ingredients that writers need to make an interesting story.

Most of the sex I experienced in Aphrodite Mode isn't all that memorable. It takes time for partners to learn how to truly satisfy one another, and many of the men I'm meeting still think of

women's bodies as a version of their own and don't appear interested in knowing the difference. And if my partners find sex with a
tall woman unusual, no one says so. When I began my novel about
Anna Swan, the writer Hugh MacLennan told me she must have
had giant organisms (*sic*), but his endearing malapropism spoke
more to his lack of knowledge of women's bodies than to the reality of women's sexual responses.

I encouraged the steady stream of boyfriends so I could say to
my inner critic, *See, I'm desirable, after all.* My posse of boyfriends
may sound counterintuitive, because I felt overwhelmed during my
twenties when men began wanting my attention. But that was then
and this is now. Not only do I seek male attention as validation, I'm
enjoying every moment of my new fun-loving mode.

Good lord, so you still need validation at forty-four? my inner
critic grumbles. *You're taking a long time to grow up, aren't you?*

How could it be otherwise? Don't most women have lifelong
tussles with their bodies?

*Oh, now you're going to have a pity party and bring up all those
teenage sock hops where you sat on the sidelines?*

I don't want to dwell on those teenage days, but yeah, I'm
probably still carrying around a schoolgirl perception of my
appearance.

*Well, guess what? You aren't a fifties teenager anymore. You'd bet-
ter catch up to yourself! You don't want to live on Channel 2 forever,
do you?*

Hmm . . . You know what, maybe I do!

A family member persuades me to read Casanova's book *The
Memoirs of Jacques Casanova de Seingalt,* and I'm fascinated by
its suspenseful account of his escape from the Leads, a Venetian

prison. In fact, the more I learn about the eighteenth-century vagabond the more it's clear he wasn't a heartless predator but someone in thrall to women. In her book *Casanova: The Man Who Really Loved Women*, psychoanalyst Lydia Flem wrote that Casanova understood women and saw them as intelligent companions whose conversations he enjoyed. He never broke up with them. Instead, he brokered a mutual separation and stayed their friend afterwards.

Lydia Flem believes he was addicted to women's love because his mother, a beautiful Venetian actress, painfully neglected him when he was a sickly boy. In his memoir, he admits he has loved women to the point of frenzy.

In a novel I later wrote about him, *What Casanova Told Me*, I put forward the idea that the task of the lover is to find the ideal in a real human being. Find the ideal in the real, an older and wiser Casanova confides in my story about his last great love affair with an American Puritan woman. Don't waste time yearning for a non-existent perfection. In other words, it's easy to appreciate who someone is when you don't expect them to be perfect.

I extrapolated my view of Casanova from my own romantic experiences because, like him, my younger self used to suffer from hopelessly idealizing romantic partners. Of course, I didn't idealize anyone deliberately. Nothing in love or friendship works that simply.

Even though I'm enjoying the excitement of the romantic chase, the novelty of a new person, and the thrill of being sought after, I'm still keeping an eye out for a potential partner. And although my romances rarely last more than a few weeks, I imagine I'm in love with each of my boyfriends—likely an unconscious dodge that lets me ignore the disapproval of women like my mother.

During this period of my life, the weight of men's traditional power isn't something I experience. If freedom is gendered, then I'm truly experiencing the way many men live, unrestricted by maternal diktat about putting others first. Once, in a Mykonos bar, a young Italian tourist tries to corner me in an empty room off the dance floor, but reading his intent, I quickly move away. My size acts as a deterrent, and perhaps men sense I'm ready to fight back. I don't hesitate to act if they physically threaten me or other women, and my anger often overtakes me. My daughter remembers a drunken man threatening us on a Toronto street when she was ten. If you take a step closer, I'll kill you, I screamed. He reeled backwards and ran off.

3.

No man tries to assault me during those years in New York. And for a brief time, with my financial success, and what remains of my youth, I can come and go as I please; I can choose who to love and for how long. I live on my own dime and I enjoy the company of men. Suddenly, I'm free to appreciate them as people rather than being cowed or feeling disadvantaged. For the first time in my life, I'm seeing a man as an individual instead of a generic representative of the male gender, even if they're still seeing me more generically than I like.

I slept my way into seeing men as people, I tell the young male journalist at *Mirabella* a few years later when my novel *The Wives of*

Bath comes out. It's an outrageous thing to say, and I blush when I read myself saying it in an American magazine, but it's the truth.

That I'm capable of moving so freely in the world is obviously connected to the reduction of childcare. I still see my daughter regularly for weekends and holidays but I don't have the daily job of looking after a teenager. The impact of having less domestic responsibility isn't lost on me. I have no one else to worry about. I am my own ward, giving myself the nutrients I need.

Now that I'm travelling more and going on book tours in other countries, men crop up everywhere. Some are lovers, some are just suitors, and some are friends. Soon there are too many men to count: the Greek Canadian bank teller in Toronto; a childhood boyfriend who lives out west; a glassblower in Athens who likes to talk philosophy with me; the twenty-something American travel agent who sends me on a tour of the Greek Islands; the Armenian nightclub owner in Amsterdam; the Cockney accountant in London (the only man not younger than me); and, for some reason, three men who all drive motorcycles.

Despite the other men who come and go in my life, Bobby is different. He is even more elusive than me, and that puts him at the top of my list. I fantasize about spending my life with him.

Bobby and the race box

1.

Bobby and I enjoy being together but he has wanderlust and, despite the expensive bike, he has no money except what he makes from writing occasional articles about his travel adventures. When I move to New York City for the winter of 1991, I invite him to join me in my sublet apartment, knowing he won't be able to pay his half of the rent. He's poor by choice. I've taken a tenured university job for financial security, but he eschews regular jobs and lives as frugally as possible.

He comes willingly, with one caveat: He insists I be in New York when he arrives because without me, he thinks the doorman won't let him in. Otherwise, he would be a Black man in a white neighbourhood and that makes him a suspicious character.

I'm beginning to appreciate the pressures he lives under as a young Black man in America. As a white person, I can't expect to ever experience how racial bigotry feels. I was born in a country where 3.5 percent of the population is Black, compared to 13.4 percent in the United States, and no Black families lived in Midland while I was growing up. The biggest cultural fights were between the Protestant English speakers and the French-speaking Catholics.

In New York, America's racial politics are often in your face. Roles feel pre-determined, no matter who you are. One afternoon, on a packed New York subway train, a group of teenagers, both Black and white, are playing a boom box so loudly I can't hear myself think. The other passengers bow their heads, grimacing. Nobody says anything. Everybody looks tense. A decade before, a white man named Bernhard Goetz got away with a short sentence after shooting four Black youths who swarmed him on a New York subway train. He was later sued successfully by one of the youths for millions of dollars. Minutes pass. Finally, I ask the kid holding the boom box if he would mind turning it down a little. I add that I like hip hop. People's heads jerk around to see who spoke. You like our music? he asks.

Yes, I like it a lot. But the volume is a bit high.

There's an awkward pause. Then he nods, smiling, and turns it down. The people near me visibly relax. My naivete helped me this time. Next time, I'll be too self-conscious to make personal requests in an over-crowded New York subway car. Next time, I'll be in the race box like everyone else.

2.

It's Martin Luther King Jr. Day in America and Bobby has stripped to his boxers and now stands in the middle of the living room in my apartment on Thirteenth Street, swinging a golf club in a hilarious imitation of the golf champion Jack Nicklaus. He's probably drawing eyeballs from people in the windows of other apartments in the high-rises you can see from our apartment window, and maybe he's clowning around to protect himself from the sadness that comes with the national holiday, which commemorates King's memory.

I'm laughing at his goofy behaviour and trying not to act as if I'm crazy about him. Which I am. Infatuated. Totally smitten and trying my best not to idealize Bobby. What he wants out of our relationship isn't clear, and it's too early to know what is going to happen between us.

He and I have just come back from having drinks with some writer friends who were at the Bread Loaf workshop with us.

It was a fun meal in the Village, although most of the time we move in different circles. Before the internet, with its emphasis on accessible language, there was more difference between the world of literary fiction authors like me and the world of non-fiction writers like Bobby, who were already addressing readers in a direct, colloquial way.

We tease each other, and sometimes we argue, and back in my apartment that evening our joking around eventually switches to a discussion of racial politics.

If you were walking along the New York sidewalk late at night and saw me coming, he says, you would cross over to the other side of the street. And that's racist, he adds, glowering at me.

I'm surprised to hear him say this because he usually avoids talking about racism with anyone. Although it's hard to imagine now, identity politics didn't exist like they do now and the early nineties were a less polarized time. But racism in America was real and even though Bobby and I downplayed its influence, its impact on us, especially Bobby, was real too.

However, Bobby's views on race are surprisingly generous. He has faith in the innate goodness of the American people, as he puts it. He likes to say if whites and Blacks knew each other better they would like one another and stop fearing someone because they have a different skin colour.

That evening, I can guess where he's going with his comment about seeing someone like him on a street late at night, but I'm not prepared to let him take his sudden bad mood out on me. So I point out that I would be right to cross to the other side of the road, because I need to protect myself.

Most of the crime in this part of town comes from young men, I add. That's why I would cross to the other side of the street whether the young man coming from the opposite direction was white or Black. So it's not racist, Bobby, it's an act of self-preservation.

No, it's racist, Bobby says. He puts on his jeans and gives me another glowering look.

I imitate his furious glare and blow some raspberries, and we both burst out laughing.

That night I dream about getting lost in the New York subway system. I'm out on a godforsaken railway track in Long Island, going nowhere and staring in bewilderment at the marshy inlets that fly by the train window. It's spring. The maple and oak trees are out in leaf and everything is green and pulsing with energy. I'm frustrated because I can't find Bobby. I'm supposed to make a connection at the next station but I don't know which train is the right one to take me back to the city where he is waiting.

3.

Bobby is determined to defy the constraints America places on him as a Black man. Walking along the New York sidewalks, he refuses to step out of the way when people approach, and he reaches for my arm so I don't step out of the way either, even though my habit of Canadian politeness means I often forget what he expects me to do and step aside.

We share our ambitions about getting ahead in the New York publishing world. It has started to open its doors to both of us. Bobby's publisher is eager for him to write more books, and I've met a Knopf editor, Jenny McPhee, who will publish *The Wives of Bath*.

Thinking back, I'm laughably WASP and uptight. He likes to hang loose, as he puts it, and our relationship is an interesting mix of gender scripts. Bobby is better at owning up to his foibles and vulnerabilities, while I'm still locked into an attempt to be macho, keeping my feelings of hurt and frustration tucked out of sight. Big girls don't cry, as the song says.

He encourages me to write a non-fiction book I'm considering, titled *In the Country of Men*. We talk about my project, which would deal with an independent woman's view of men, although I never end up writing it. Cultural changes are moving too quickly and there are already books on the subject by writers like the philosopher James Hillman and poet Robert Bly, the author of *Iron John: A Book About Men*. For my part, I encourage the book projects Bobby is developing even though these projects usually involve travel expeditions that take him away from New York City and me. Every few weeks I return to Toronto to see my daughter and make arrangements about my next teaching year, and Bobby does his thing of hopping on his bike to take a trip to some distant part of America.

Guess it's time to find out what's going on out there, Bobby would call, heading for the door.

He's like a twentieth-century version of a frontier scout every time he jumps on his motorcycle and roars out of the city, the fringe on his leather jacket blowing wildly about in the wind.

However, despite the warmth of our bond, I have no experience of the world Bobby comes from, and it isn't until the day I visit him in Harlem that the pernicious extent of American racism hits home. It's the year I'm back in Toronto teaching creative writing students, and Bobby has rented an apartment in the historic neighbourhood of Sugar Hill. The residential area with its notable architecture has gone through a cycle of deterioration since the forties, and in the early nineties it's still struggling, a situation that Bobby later writes about in one of his books.

When I get off at my subway stop, a middle-aged white man dressed in a business suit rushes over and shouts in my face. What are you doing in Harlem? he asks. You shouldn't be here alone.

I tell him I am visiting a friend, and he orders me to go back downtown. I ignore him and walk on, passing two Black men washing a car while music plays. The water from their hoses trickles by my sneakered feet, and nearby, two kids are singing along as they float sticks in the stream. I am the only white person around. I think of Bobby, Black in the New York publishing world, where almost everyone is white.

I walk by more groups of people laughing and talking. Despite the vacant lots and the rundown tenements, the streets radiate a magnetic vitality. The life force seems to bubble up from the asphalt beneath my feet.

I sit waiting for Bobby on the steps of his new home, a four-storey apartment house in West Harlem. As usual, he is late, and Black women hurrying up the steps with their groceries stare at me in surprise and I smile and nod and try to look inoffensive. By the time Bobby arrives, apologizing repeatedly, I am in a daze. I let him show me around his apartment, his first home away from St. Louis, while I struggle with how to tell him what I feel. No words come.

That afternoon, I finally understand he is more than the romantic longings I projected onto the glamorous figure in Vermont standing by his motorcycle, holding up his book, while giggling young women took his photograph. I have done to him what numerous callow men have done to me—seen him as a vehicle for my needs instead of recognizing his depth as a person—and I realize with a prickle of sadness that I am only beginning to understand the problems caused by Black oppression in the United States. He is writing highly personal non-fiction books about what it means to be Black in America after centuries of slavery. In some respects, his approach to his work has a few parallels with the feminist quest for respect and autonomy I express in my fiction, but white feminists like myself are rapidly becoming part of the establishment while Black writers have the burden of racial prejudice to deal with. His life work is an all-encompassing literary project, a Jonah-in-the-whale-sized project. If we stay together, it would be hard not to slip into a supportive feminine role. What if, together, we weren't able to make it work financially? Maybe I would end up supporting us both because he's determined, at this stage in his career, not to accept office jobs with financial security. What would happen to my own work? Was I selfless enough to be his companion and enabler, to put his project ahead of mine? I know the answer. I've always known. I'm too independent now to limit myself to being a man's helpmate. If I have a partner, I need that partner to help me.

However, it isn't just the fear of being submerged by the demanding scope of his life project. In Toronto, I have a teenage daughter and a tenure-track teaching position and I'm not prepared to put either the daughter or the security of my job aside and live a nomadic life with him. We recognize each other as free spirits, although his thirst for aloneness and adventure is greater than mine. He's eleven years younger and his first interest is the open road, not settling down. I've been fooling myself with a romantic fantasy about another person that doesn't take into account their life experience.

A kite tail of insights

A few months later, I am doing holotropic breathing as I sit meditating in my Toronto home. Holotropic breathwork is the practice of breathing rapidly and evenly so you get in touch with unconscious parts of yourself.

While I sit, breathing quickly, an image appears of my chest as a pioneer quilt. The patches are made up of many different brightly coloured pieces of fabric and there is a large dark hole over the part of the quilt that covers my heart.

I'm seeing the psychic hole left by my two childhood wounds—a remote father and my size. As I continue to breathe rapidly, patches of fabric start to creep in the direction of the hole until the dark space is completely covered by the quilt. Slowly the image fades and the thought comes that I'll be all right if I don't find a loving partner and have to live alone for the rest of my life. The insight feels light, without judgment. So be it, I tell myself.

What a moment! Blam—BANG, THWIP, KTANG, SHAZAM—that's the noise of my psyche experiencing a powerful insight. The insight is about myself and the men I've been seeing. None of them are holding me back; the box is my craving for male love. I still enjoy it but I don't need it the way I used to. I'm more interested in being out in the world looking for what makes me feel more joyful, more playful and creative, more like myself.

Then, like colourful ribbons on the tail of a kite, a stream of other insights dance into view, including an astonishing new realization: falling in love with ambivalent men is a good way to hide the truth that I'm ambivalent about intimacy too. In fact, I fear it. That's why Bobby and I are perfect for each other. Oops, were perfect for each other.

Not long after this meditation, I meet Patrick Crean at a meditation retreat. He publishes fiction by my friend, the Canadian writer Barbara Gowdy, and after the retreat, she holds a dinner party so we can get to know each other. She tells me he's crazy about me, but during the meal he doesn't look my way, so I think he isn't interested. Later he tells me he had been so dazzled that he couldn't meet my eye.

Although I'm still intent on living part-time in New York, I feel drawn to him. He's a tender, serious-minded man who spent his boyhood in Paris, France, so he has an elegant approach to women and sexuality. He also has a private mystical side that I find interesting. He makes astrological charts of his friends and reads spiritual classics like *The Tibetan Book of the Dead* and *The Secret Doctrine* by Madame Helena Blavatsky. Of course, he has his wounds too. He has just left an unhappy marriage. He is five foot eight but his height doesn't matter. He understands me. He is a book editor and my daughter likes him. He's the first boyfriend of mine that she fully accepts after my divorce from her father. He also likes her. Being with him feels like coming home.

In my journal, I write down sixteen reasons why I like Patrick, including our ability to create "a zone of pleasure" that reinforces our mutual creativity. He likes solitude and togetherness in the same amounts I do. Most of the men I know either want too much togetherness or too little, and it's hard to find a balance that works for me. Getting together with Patrick falls into a natural rhythm, and he quickly gets rid of the ex-boyfriends who are still hanging around, telling them brusquely that he is seeing me now.

I assume too much responsibility for the other person in my relations with them, I write to him in a letter. When I get close I think I'm betraying the other person if I want to be alone to write, and so for me intimacy has always been a little sticky, with problems of guilt and feelings of suffocation on my side.

When I tell Bobby about Patrick, he comes to the sunlit Chelsea apartment I've rented and tries to talk me out of my new relationship, but he and I are starting to move in different orbits, getting on with our lives in a way that leaves no room for each other.

Only a few months before the Harlem visit with Bobby, sitting in a coffee shop with a friend, I burst into tears after reading a *New York Times* story about a ten-year-old girl who was found homeless in Brooklyn.

My friend asks, Do you think it's time to go back to your people? I answer no, but he's put his finger on the reason for my sadness. Although I admire the dynamism of American culture, I've never been able to understand its belief that if you succeed, you have done it by yourself, and if you don't succeed, well, too bad for you, you have only yourself to blame. As much as I wish they were able to see the mutual benefits of a stronger social security net, their faith in winners and losers feels unshakeable. It's the reason why some of the Americans I meet wholeheartedly reject universal health care. They don't want to pay for health care for the poor even though they, too, would receive the same financial help with their medical bills.

The failure is surprising for a practical people like the Americans. And the cruelty implied in the moral judgment that being poor is your own fault is heartbreaking.

Without universal health care and a fair minimum wage, thousands of Americans live in situations like the ten-year-old Brooklyn girl whose story made me cry. In the New York coffee shop with my friend, I realize he is right; it's time to go back home, where people don't live in a perfect world either, but where, for all the failings of my culture, at least people understand that we need to be able to depend on each other in order to get through the winter together. Soon after that conversation, I leave New York City and, seven months later, I move in with Patrick.

Falling out of a myth

In 1993, two Canadian writers and I stage a show in New York titled *An Evening of Sexual Gothic*. (The show was originally billed as *An Evening of Sexual Gothic with Canadian Writers*, but the board members of Symphony Space broke out laughing when they heard the title because they didn't think Canadians could do something so interesting and the title was shortened.)

I'm still traveling to New York off and on and renting rooms at the Hotel Chelsea, which is world famous for its Bohemian hospitality. The walls of the lobby are hung with paintings by unknown artists who live at the hotel, and if you're a writer or an artist you might get a discount on the price. That's because the hotel staff is impressed if making art is your vocation, your credo, or even just a hobby. Their attitude evokes the tradition of the poverty-stricken genius who suffers for their art, an obvious version of the penniless Christian monk, but it's unusual in a city like New York.

Every time I walk through the hotel door, the hotel manager, Jerry Weinstein, says, Welcome home, Ms. Swan. I have a room at the Chelsea when we put on *An Evening of Sexual Gothic*. I'm in suite 829, which belonged to the late American author Thomas Wolfe. Thomas, not Tom, I tell young friends. It has ten-foot ceilings, a working fireplace, and antique wooden shutters that I close at night.

An Evening of Sexual Gothic has been cleverly designed and marketed by freelance promoter Judith Keenan, who has successfully publicized many of my novels. It features an excerpt from my novel *The Wives of Bath* as well as short stories by Barbara Gowdy and the late Eric McCormack. We also put it on at Toronto's Hart House and a Chicago library. During the event, actors read from our books and then, dressed in chain mail—shades of my days as a performance artist, Barbara and I talked with Eric about the meaning of *sexual gothic*, a term for fiction that expresses uneasiness about the human body. That night, we theorize that the body is the site of conflicting passions in the same way that medieval castles are used as settings in traditional Gothic novels. A critic in the *Village Voice* calls it a most provocative and literary evening. Soon afterwards, I fly back to Toronto.

I've been fascinated by America and the way Americans act out their ideas through celebrities and media personalities. And now I'm tumbling headfirst out of a myth, coming to the end of my fantastical dream in which I'm propelled head over heels across the Catskills while Rip Van Winkle, the headless horseman, and Henry Hudson's ghost ship fly by. Unlike the show business giant Anna Swan and her husband, the Kentucky Giant, I'm not staying in America. I'm moving on.

Part Four

THE SACRED GROVE

1.

The highway from the Athens airport is thick with fast-moving cars. While we speed along, the taxi driver pulls alongside another cab and holds out his hand. As the two taxis race side by side down the road, the other driver hands him a lit cigarette. Noticing my frown in his rear-view mirror, my driver shrugs at my disapproval and announces that he can't take me into Athens. Why? I demand incredulously.

He says a strike has just shut down the city. I don't believe him and I sit there fuming. I dislike everything about him—from his craggy, smirking face to the calloused toes poking out of his worn-out sandals pressing down on the accelerator. I especially dislike the arrogance in his deep raspy voice, which I'll discover is typical of many older Greek men. I order him to pull over to the side of the road and let me out. I want to get as far away as possible from him and his chaotic city with its endless jumble of dirty white concrete houses and flat-roofed apartment buildings.

You can't get out here! He gestures at the traffic streaming by us.

I'm getting out, I repeat. And I'm not going to pay you. He

looks disbelieving until his eyes catch mine in the mirror. Sighing and shaking his head, he pulls over.

I guess he's thinking, *Damn American tourist woman,* and I'm ready to ream him out for not knowing the difference between his Canadian and American customers. To my surprise, he suggests I stay at his cousin's hotel in the harbour of Piraeus. It's cheap and clean and that way I can wait until the next morning to go into Athens. By then the strike will be over.

The sound of his new reasonable voice calms me. It's 1989, and I'm still teaching one year in Toronto and going back and forth to New York the year I'm not teaching. I've just come from London, England, where the grisly massacre of students in Tiananmen Square plays nightly on the television set at the women's residence in Crosby Hall. The owner of his cousin's hotel probably gives him a cut for bringing in business, but it's my first time in Greece. I have nowhere else to go and the thought of sleep is suddenly appealing, so I tell the driver to take me there.

The hotel is exactly as my taxi driver described it. A clean, modest four-storey building by the harbour. In its sparsely furnished lobby, a few older Greek men sit smoking cigarettes on wooden-backed chairs and directing lecherous glances my way. I'm in full Aphrodite attire this afternoon, dressed in shorts and a matching white halter top. My blond hair has been done in braids for the heat.

My room turns out to be as clean as the lobby. In the morning, newly rested, I meet the cousin of the taxi driver, a slender young man with a gentle, inquiring manner who tells me he has graduated that spring from the University of Athens.

Unfortunately, he says the strike is still on and I'll have to stay at his hotel for another day. I groan. One more day? Smiling sympathetically, the young man adds, Why don't you take a tour of the islands near Piraeus? You will like it. I promise you.

With no real alternative, I agree, and he walks me down to the hectic scene at the harbour where a small Greek ferry is boarding passengers for the islands of Hydra, Aegina, and Spetses. I buy my ticket, and in minutes, I'm seated in the lounge that displays the same cheap but clean appearance as the small hotel. As the soothing rhythms of the pop song "Never on a Sunday" drift through the ship's sound system, I order a Nescafé and a plate of spanakopita.

The steady motion of the boat feels reassuring. I've always liked being on the water, and after I finish breakfast, I rush out to the deck to watch Piraeus disappearing behind the ferry, "Never on a Sunday" still piping overhead. The harbour with its huge white cruise liners, its Greek ferries, the backpackers struggling with their burdens, and the figures on the docks toting baggage or carrying briefcases—all that once was so close now disappears.

The sunlight startles me. It's hot even though it's only June. Lines from a poem tug at my memory, and I realize I'm seeing the golden sunlight that Homer writes about in *The Odyssey*. It sparkles in the air and turns the surface of the Aegean a rich navy blue and turquoise.

So this is Greece, I tell myself. I can't stop smiling. Henry Miller called Greece the "sacred precinct" in his non-fiction classic *The Colossus of Maroussi*. Marvellous things happen to one in Greece, the master of sexist braggadocio wrote in that book. *Marvellous good things that can happen to one nowhere else on earth.*

Like Miller, I'm in my early forties when I come. I've been

hired to teach a writing workshop on Skyros, a Greek island in the Aegean Sea, and a month in Greece promises to be a peaceful antidote to the harshness of America and its social problems.

2.

The next day the strike in Athens ends and in the early afternoon, I move to the Athens Gate Hotel, where I have reservations. That night I watch the sun drop into the Aegean from the hotel's roof-top balcony. Its fading light turns the mountains around Athens a soft lilac hue and deepens the colours of rose and mauve in the cloudless sky. Nearby Mount Lycabettus is glowing a radiant shade of amethyst. Closer still, on a high limestone crag, is the Acropolis. I've an unrestricted view of its tall, ivory columns lit up by the Sound and Light Show while below stretches the end-less bricolage of the city, its houses and low apartment buildings scattered in all directions like thousands upon thousands of white dice.

From the vantage point of the roof, I understand that Athens lies in a plain between the mountains and the sea, and I'm amazed by how close I feel to nature. There is Homer's wine-dark Aegean, and here the purpled hills, and although I sit under electric lamps on the balcony and can hear the whine of motor scooters on the streets below, I imagine I can taste the salt brine of the sea only a mile or two away.

It's my first inkling that the Greeks live closer to nature and are more attuned to the seasons than North Americans and Euro-peans. The country has never industrialized in the traditional

Western sense and it offers instead a bracing simplicity. It's secure in the knowledge that it established the brilliance of its intellectual culture several millennia ago, an achievement so irrefutable that there is every reason to relax and sink into the physical pleasures of the day. Instead of full-bodied California reds, there's retsina, the yellow alcohol seasoned with the sap of pine trees, and instead of steak there is plenty of fresh seafood, not to mention the baking dry heat, and the inviting caldron of blue sea and sky.

That night, surrounded in four directions by the splendour of the Mediterranean evening, I start to laugh. I'm far too predictable. When I enter a new place, I wonder why I've come. Then, as my defensiveness crumbles, I begin to appreciate what I see around me. It seems I need to say no before I can say yes.

A few minutes later, a young American walks over and introduces himself as a travel agent from New Jersey. He says he is struck by how much I resemble his stepmother, with whom he had once been in love.

These sorts of surprising confessions, friendly and straightforward (and often a come-on), happen regularly in Greece. In such a natural setting, and with the inhabitants' lack of pretension, it feels as if many of the threats to human life are invisible, or at least temporarily suspended. I'm still in Aphrodite Mode, and that evening in Athens it seems I'm stumbling onto something important: my body feels at home in Greece. I don't need much here to enjoy being alive. Some clean clothes, a glass of Greek wine, and a welcoming bowl of horiatiki salata, filled to the top with fresh tomatoes and cucumbers and local feta cheese and olive oil all mixed together in the satisfactory way that only the Greeks are able to do.

So when the young American asks if he can join me, what else can I say but yes?

Greece is a pleasure box

1.

I thought by this time I'd be through with boxes, but boxes are inescapable. No matter what I do, they surround me—narrow boxes and generous boxes and oppressive boxes that you don't see because they exist in your head. Boxes that are physical realities out there in the world and psychological boxes that offer a framework you need to grow and live by. The truth is that a bad box is a framework that holds you back from growing into the person you need to be, while a good box holds you lightly but not loosely, instead of squeezing the life force out of you, metaphorically speaking.

Boxes are the "there there" in our lives, to borrow a phrase from the writer Gertrude Stein, so I don't need to escape something just because it's a box, do I?

I'm not a psychiatrist or even a well-meaning counsellor of the sort you might find in your local high school giving misguided advice.

I'm box savvy, and perhaps you are, too, but that doesn't stop us from occasionally finding ourselves in a box that turns into some hellish dark space that we need to cycle out of if we want to keep breathing.

To these fears, I can only say that in my experience, boxes become more visible as we journey through time, since we're equipped with older eyes that notice things we were too young to see before. So have courage, any of you who, like me, find yourselves living in the land of many boxes. If we look carefully, we can find paths that lead us through and out.

Boxes have mattered to me because the story I've been telling is one of not fitting the cultural spaces I've been given. And what exactly didn't I fit? Many of the conventional boxes of my culture, not only the traditional boxes for women but the traditional boxes for men too. However, if my body doesn't fit the gender scripts I grew up with, why bother trying? It only took me to my mid-forties to discover that it's easier to be my own norm.

As for boxes, now is the moment to say what many people already know—Greece is a pleasure box. Western writers and artists and visitors have been extolling its humanity and its beauty for a few centuries now, and here I am, about to do it too.

ON MY FIRST day in Athens, to my surprise, my inner critic and I feel aligned, and on a street near my hotel I stop to pluck an orange from one of the many orange trees lining the boulevard. The orange is sweet-tasting and I gulp it down. Who knew I was so eager for the simple thrill of picking a fruit from a nearby tree? And who would guess that orange trees could grow on a city street? Obviously, the Greeks know the physical world with its sensory pleasures is there to be enjoyed, and I can't help wondering why it's taken me so long to get here.

The next afternoon, over a delicious lunch of calamari at a restaurant near my hotel, I read up on Skyros, a less touristy island in the Sporades, which is an archipelago off the east coast of

Greece. It's known for its old folk ways, like its annual goat dance when men dress up in animal skins in a ritual that some scholars link back to the days when villagers on the island worshipped Dionysius. It also happens to be the burial place of the famous World War One poet Rupert Brooke. When I travel to Skyros, I'll go to Atsitsa, a new-age resort, and teach a fiction-writing workshop. Founded by Dina Glouberman, a London psychotherapist, Atsitsa attracts people from all over the world who are looking for a wholistic vacation where they can take courses in windsurfing, yoga, theatre improvisation, singing, photography, art, and, of course, creative writing.

A few days later, after a taxi ride from the Skyros airport, I find myself looking at a cluster of old stone buildings lining a promontory on a remote bay. The scent of resin from the nearby pine forest drifts through the air, and all around me, cicadas are singing in the intense summer heat. The resort is overcrowded, so a staff member leads me to the taverna at the bottom of the hill on Atsitsa Bay. It's a small hike from the central campus, and at first, I feel slighted that I haven't been given a room in one of the stone houses where most of the staff are quartered. But it doesn't take me very long to realize that my lodgings mean I can hold my writing workshop on the taverna's large porch, the sea glittering behind the wild reeds growing on the beach. It sounds more relaxing than sitting inside a stone house on the promontory.

In the morning, I meet my class in the taverna for the first time. They are mostly tourists from London, England, except for a young male playwright from New Zealand; a Scottish woman who makes her living as a freelance journalist; and a retired history professor from an American Midwest college along with others whose names have melted into the blur of the hundreds upon hundreds of faces I've encountered in my decades of teaching writing.

I'm worried that their stories are going to be a version of the work I get from undergraduates at Toronto's York University. In those years, student fiction often relies on highly stylized passages of physical violence, which is what happens when people see too many American crime shows and the glamorized scenes they write bear no relation to real life. As a reporter, I've witnessed actual crime scenes, and what my undergraduate students write about doesn't describe the ugliness of what happens when people try to kill or brutalize each other.

In order to get them to write convincingly about violence, each September, I take my class of undergraduate students to the Toronto morgue, where a public relations officer greets them warmly before he launches into his spiel. It begins with the chilling statement that every corpse brings a story with it. Then he leads them through a grotesque slideshow about the cadavers of Toronto's most interesting or well-known murders. To cap his talk, he also plays a terrifying recording of a serial killer explaining his MO. The one godsend: the man doesn't show us dead bodies in their drawers.

No matter how much I warn them, a few students will smoke marijuana beforehand and come thinking they're in for some ghoulish fun only to find they need to leave soon after the morgue tour has begun.

At the Atsitsa taverna, I take one look at my students' eager, middle-aged faces and decide against telling them about the morgue tour. Instead, I give them an exercise from my bag of creative writing tricks and ask them to do the bad-writing assign-ment, which involves writing a one-page story using as many clichés and melodramatic tropes as possible. There are snorts and laugh-ter and cries of: She can't be serious. I laugh too before I explain that the exercise is a shortcut. Although everyone resists at first, it will quickly teach them to recognize these mistakes when they do their short stories or novel openings.

As my students start writing, I'm aware of us being watched by a balding man with a large, well-shaped head like the ones you see on Greek statues from classical times. He's sitting at another table listening to us as he smokes one cigarette after another. I don't know his name but I've noticed him going down the hall to his room in the taverna, which is four doors away from mine. When he sees me looking his way, he catches my eye and smiles.

I respond with a wan smile because I don't want him interrupt-ing the workshop. Turning back to the class, I ask the students to read their one page of purple prose out loud to each other. Two of them who didn't take me seriously have scribbled down earnest, well-meaning fictional accounts that I jokingly announce get a "failed" mark. Everyone laughs and claps.

The others have done what I asked and purposefully stacked their accounts with howlers like "baby blues," "grab the bull by the horns," "plenty of fish in the sea," "every cloud has a silver lining," and "you can't judge a book by its cover." Luckily, for the purposes of my workshop, the list of clichés in the English lan-guage is endless.

The students laugh and clap again when they hear the clichés, and so do I. The New Zealand playwright has managed to insert the famous melodramatic phrase "It was a dark and stormy night" into his exercise, and I announce that he's getting an A because that phrase has been synonymous with bad writing ever since 1830, when the English novelist Edward Bulwer-Lytton used it to open his florid, overwritten novel *Paul Clifford*.

The class cheers. Now that the atmosphere is more relaxed and I have their full attention, I consider assigning an exercise about the importance of specific, concrete language. To that end, I sometimes ask students to describe me in specific detail without using vague general adjectives like *tall* and *blond*. After getting over their nervousness or glee, they usually do the assignment well. It's a useful way to point out the difference between saying *a big room* and saying *a large classroom with a low ceiling and walls designed by architects to withstand earthquakes . . .*

There's always the risk someone will make a rude comment, although nobody does. Getting a room of young people to *hang on your every word* . . . (yikes, a cliché!) Teaching *does wonders* (yikes again—a second cliché) for your confidence. If you can interest a room of bored and distracted undergraduates, chances are you can hold the attention of anyone. In my case, it also satisfies a longing left over from my childhood, the wish to be admired instead of attracting thoughtless or mean remarks about my height.

However, the exercise requires a degree of trust which hasn't been established yet with my Atsitsa students, so I start talking about the old writing workshop axiom of showing and telling. The two terms describe the difference between stories that summarize the experience of the characters and those that put the reader in the experience of the characters as they are experiencing it.

The best way of explaining showing to a class of amateur writers is for me to act it out, so I tell them the story of meeting the Irish

Giant, who billed himself as the Tallest Man in the World when I interviewed him at the Niagara Falls Guinness World Records Museum. I visited the museum in 1978 to hear him talk, during the days when I was researching my novel about Anna Swan.

In the Atsitsa taverna, I start explaining what I mean by showing not telling. This is telling or summarizing, I tell the workshop: *I interviewed the Tallest Man in the World at the Niagara Falls Guinness World Records Museum, and after his talk, he asked me for a date so I ran away.*

And this is the beginning of a longer storytelling version: *The giant comes out of the Guinness museum, his head higher than the marquee. He extends a huge rubbery hand and says: Sue, I don't get to meet tall girls like you every day. What are you doing after my show?*

I have a boyfriend back in Toronto, I reply, trying to sound firm. He laughs as we walk into the Guinness museum and says, I bet you say that to all the boys.

There are hoots of appreciation, although some of the women at our table look anxious on my behalf. So I mimic what the giant says to his audience in the museum theatre about his lonely personal life in Dublin, how he feels tired of going on the road and giving speeches and opening shopping plazas for a living, and how all his furniture is normal size, including his Mini Minor, which hurts him to sit in, and how he likes to have everything the same size as the things normal people use.

Then I speak in my own voice and describe how the giant's confession makes me remember my own need to wear clothes that were too small for me, and how our attempt to be like everyone else is a child's protest against reality, a plea and a hope that we won't be persecuted for being different.

And then I mimic the voice of someone in the crowded lecture hall who asks the giant why he isn't married. He catches my eye, I tell the workshop, and says: I haven't met the right girl. But things could be changing . . .

In front of my students, I act out how I ran out of the door of the museum theatre and how he ran after me, his giant feet making big whacking sounds on the wooden floor of the hall, and how the manager of the museum grabs my arm and yanks me into his office, claiming the giant wants to see me after the last show. I tell the students how the giant bursts into the manager's office and how crestfallen he looks when I say I'm leaving and how he pleads like a little boy for a goodbye kiss until I take pity on him, and how, standing on my tiptoes, I anxiously kiss his rubbery lips before I run out the door. I describe rushing by the long line of people waiting to see the giant's next show and how a roar of excitement goes through the crowd, and how, when I hear the sound, I turn around and see the giant coming out of the museum; he's rushing towards me, his long arms stretched out in my direction as he begs in a pitiful voice for me to come back. And then his manager appears and the crowd makes a long *oh* sound of disappointment as his manager drags the giant back into the museum in order to stop the people from seeing him before his next show, and how at last I'm able to shout in a calm voice: Goodbye, Bill.

The class sits goggle-eyed when my story finishes, and we spend the rest of the afternoon discussing how my attempt to interview the Irish Giant quickly turned someone like me, who has spent hours researching the lives of giants, into a child running from an ogre in a fairy tale.

As the class ends, and the students leave the taverna chattering and smiling, the bald-headed man comes over and asks if he can buy me a glass of ouzo. It's a viscous Greek liquor high in alcoholic content. He says his name is Achilles and he's a glass-blower from Athens, which I instantly take to mean that he's one of the aggressive Greek shopkeepers who flog glass trinkets to tourists. However, I don't say that to him.

In the next breath he tells me that he is an ex-heroin addict, and he's come to Atsitsa to see if its theatre workshops can help him with the recovery from his addiction. Curious, I accept his offer, and he begins to ask me questions about what he has overheard. He says he can teach someone glass-blowing techniques because the techniques are well tested, but he wonders how anyone can teach a person to be a writer.

I've thought about that question, so I tell Achilles that nobody can teach anyone to be a writer. A person has to want to write and be willing to learn the craft by putting in hours of writing. However, the life of a writer requires a certain temperament that allows you to sit in a room for hours working on a piece of prose. I've had brilliant students who hate the solitude of writing and go on to publish nothing, and less talented students who go on to successful careers because they can cope with being solitary. So my exercises are created to give tips about craft to future novelists and to make better readers out of those who won't take up a professional writing career. He lights up a Karelia Light, a Greek cigarette, and nods approvingly.

2.

It turns out there is no need to talk my Atsitsa students out of writing about violence in a faux stylized manner. The inescapable beauty of the turquoise Mediterranean so near at hand; the susurrus of its waves hitting the beach by the taverna where we work; the excitable chorus of the cicadas in the pine trees—all that we see and hear is so peaceful and appealing that my students can't help writing interesting stories that have nothing in common with the glitzy accounts of violence in North American crime dramas.

And every day after the class is over, Achilles and I sit at the taverna and talk. Unlike me, Achilles hasn't studied Western philosophers at university, but like many Greeks, he knows the thinkers of ancient Greece. In his lexicon, Aristotle is a fusty archivist who doesn't share Achilles's belief that the purpose of freedom is to create beauty, and Plato is a rigid idealist too taken with abstractions. The Stoics, of which Achilles is one, are his favourite. He insists they were right about happiness coming from accepting the moment as it presents itself. He is my age, forty-four, and he extends to everyone a neutral generosity that I find comforting. He also seems older because his manner is fatherly. When our conversation finishes, we usually sit in a comfortable silence staring at the sea. I have a soft spot for fatherly men, and after a few days of drinking retsina and eating mezedes, the Greek word for snacks, I start confiding what I'm learning about myself at Atsitsa while he sits like a Greek Buddha, power-smoking and listening.

The meaning of the ham sandwich

Kalinichta, kalinichta, Achilles jokes, as I start talking about my dream of making a ham sandwich. (*Kalinichta* is the Greek word for goodnight.) He chuckles as he lights up one of his Karelia cigarettes, a signal he's eager to hear my story, which starts with Virginia, the Jungian therapist who gives workshops at Atsitsa. She lives in one of the uncomfortable bamboo huts scattered beyond the stone houses on the cliff.

It is mostly young guests who sleep in them, because they can endure the hard floor and the whine of the feeble Skyros mosquitoes that gather at twilight. These guests are twenty-something tourists; Virginia is in her fifties and she says her Spartan taste means the hut and the privacy it offers are what she likes.

One night at supper, she starts talking about dreams. She says every part of a dream is part of the dreamer, so if you want to know what your dream means you need to interview each part, including the floor (if a floor exists in your dream), and you must ask questions as if the part is a person and then listen to what it has to say. The Jungian technique that treats parts of the unconscious like fictional characters makes sense to me because it resembles the way I handle my inner critic.

Virginia points out that nothing will happen if your answers are overly analytical. When you interview the dream part you must let it say the first thing that pops into your head. The first thing that pops into your head will be the right answer.

That night after my talk with Virginia, I dream about my mother. By the way, I say to Achilles, did I mention that Virginia is

willowy and blond, just like my mother? Achilles shakes his head
no and then nods appreciatively.

In the dream, my mother is showing me how to make a proper
ham sandwich when suddenly a small dark-haired woman appears
in the kitchen and says, Mrs. Swan, there are many ways to make
a ham sandwich and some of them don't include ham. The small
dark-haired woman is half my size and she exudes a ferocious energy when she addresses my mother. I'm speechless. As I stare at
the two women, my mother disappears in a puff of smoke and the
small dark-haired woman ascends into the sky and vanishes too.

The next morning, Virginia says there's no need to do a question-
and-answer with the small dark-haired woman because it's obvious
she is my anima who is providing me with life-giving wisdom to
protect me against my mother's perfectionism. Later, in my room
in the taverna, I write out a dialogue with the dream figure anyway.

> **Me to the small dark-haired woman:** Were you
>   telling my mother off in that dream?
> **Small dark-haired woman:** Not at all. I was just
>   pointing out the obvious. There are many ways
>   to reach the truth of something, and sometimes
>   the truth isn't at all what we were told it is.
> **Me:** Why are you so small if you are my anima?
> **Small dark-haired woman (laughing):** Why can't an anima
>   be small? Do you have something against short women?
> **Me:** Oh god, I'm sorry.
> **Small dark-haired woman (still laughing):** That's all
>   right. Just remember, Virginia and your mother are

not the ultimate source of knowledge about who you
are and what you want—it's you and nobody else.

When I finish telling the story of my dream, Achilles pats my
shoulder, and, smiling more broadly than usual, offers me one
of his Greek cigarettes. To my surprise, the harsh tobacco tastes
wonderful on my tongue, and together we sit smoking and staring
contentedly at the waves breaking beyond the shore. An intimacy
is growing between us. Sometimes when I'm not in the taverna,
he will send someone to fetch me so we can talk. However, I'm determined nothing romantic is going to happen. I have my eye on
Craig, the tall, good-looking Australian who teaches windsurfing.
Craig lacks the depth of someone like Achilles, but Achilles is all
of five foot six. In his favour, his stocky, well-built body is strong,
and like many Greeks, he seems comfortable in his own skin.

I can feel my heart softening towards him, and as we sit smoking,
I remind myself that he's not tall enough for me, and besides, he's a
recovering addict. Worse still, although he's a grown man, he still
lives with his mother, who keeps house for him.

About twenty minutes later, as he stubs out another cigarette,
Achilles asks me to tell him what else I'm learning at Atsitsa. By this
point, I don't need more encouragement, so I start talking about
the afternoon when the Greek army came to the Atsitsa beach.

Aphrodite and the Greek army

Yesterday afternoon, as I walk out of the sea, dripping wet in a bikini, Tim, the young New Zealand playwright, taps my shoulder

and points to the beach. The Greek army has come to swim after a military exercise, and at least forty men still in camouflage outfits are lounging on their towels, listening to their radios. As we walk towards them, the soldiers get to their feet one by one and stare in our direction.

They think you're Aphrodite rising from the sea, my student Tim whispers. When I scoff, he looks insulted. Why can't I accept his compliment gracefully? Surely, I don't still harbour a fear that the sight of my body might provoke jeers? Well, not exactly. I've given up worrying about my appearance and I'm enjoying being a woman visiting Greece, but I have no idea how a bunch of Greek soldiers will behave.

Tim grasps my arm, determined to make his point. Don't you know that your size is mythic to most men? he asks. Tim points at the soldiers, who are still looking my way. Not one of them has whistled or made a catcall. Instead, they're gazing at me in respectful silence. The soldiers' quiet respect seems to evoke an archaic time when men could appreciate a woman's appearance without resorting to degrading comments, and to my surprise, I feel as if my human body is stepping into the dimension of myth. It's as if everything I've enjoyed about Aphrodite Mode has culminated in this experience. And it's happening, imagine this if you can, beyond the realm of a Hollywood movie. The words of Henry Miller's prophecy resound in my head: If a mythic moment is going to happen to you, more often than not, it will happen to you in Greece.

I nod at the soldiers and smile as Tim and I walk off to drink beer at the taverna.

Is this the natural ending to my journey about the perils of travelling through life in a big female body? Maybe it's the ending I've been looking for in my search for self-validation, a kind of reckoning that many women undertake sooner or later in their struggles with their body. Or maybe there is more to come, I think, not knowing how true that will turn out to be.

In any case, Achilles enjoys my Aphrodite story so much he's going to tell me a story too. He says the story is not about him, it's about a friend. Yet I can't help feeling his story is about his recovery from a heroin addiction. He's secretive about how he behaved when he was an addict and it would be natural for him to want to protect himself.

Greece brings you what your unconscious needs

1.

A friend of Achilles who was suffering from depression travels to Crete to meet some friends, who have become archaeologists. They tell him to meet them near a remote village in the Lassithi Plateau, the largest plateau in Crete.

So he rents a car and goes to the village, but he can't find his friends. Nobody has seen them. Finally, an old woman in traditional Greek clothes says she thinks she saw some strangers walking around an olive grove halfway up the mountain. It's a vague direction, and the friend of Achilles starts hiking through the olive groves, but he can't find his friends. He's exhausted so he sits down on a large stone, wondering what to do. A few minutes later, his friends appear from between the olive trees. They rush over and greet him, and then they notice the crumbling stone that he has been sitting on.

His friends begin to shout in excitement and clap him on the back because he's sitting on the remains of an ancient temple. They rush him off to the nearest taverna and buy him drinks.

Without intending to help them, the friend of Achilles has led the Greek archaeologists to the ancient ruins they had been trying to find for weeks, and they insist on paying for his room and board for the rest of the week. The experience comes at a good time in the life of Achilles's friend, who had been feeling down because he felt his life was lacking in meaning.

But after the discovery of the old ruins, not only does he understand (perhaps for the first time) that he has kind and appreciative friends, he also realizes that he is the one who has brought meaning to them.

When he finishes his story, I'm stunned. Maybe Greece brings you what your unconscious needs, I blurt, repeating something said to me by someone who visited Greece. Achilles looks pleased, and he insists I take his pack of Karelia cigarettes. I shake my head. The gift of his story is enough.

On the last day of my stay at Atsitsa, he and I are standing by the buffet table at a goodbye party the resort staff has thrown for the guests. Everyone is dancing to ABBA, the Swedish rock group, and through the crowds, the tall Australian windsurfing teacher is heading my way. He waves at me, and I wave back just as one of Atsitsa's psychotherapists, a pretty dark-haired American woman, steps in front of him and leads the windsurfer teacher away from the dance floor.

Feeling frustrated, I watch them go off together, but I can't get up the energy to walk over and interrupt what is going on. Instead, I keep talking to Achilles, and the next morning, he asks me to meet him in Mykonos as soon as my teaching job is over. I've always wanted to see Mykonos, a popular tourist destination in the Cycladic Islands. So I say yes, and immediately feel anxious. Why am I agreeing to meet him on a romantic getaway? Won't I regret it? My inner critic jumps in with an answer: Of course you will, you foolish woman, haven't you learned to say no by now? You don't have to give somebody something just because they have their hand out.

Putting aside my fears, I buy a ticket on the ferry to Mykonos.

2.

It's a windy day and Greek ferries feel notoriously vulnerable in bad weather, so my nerves are already shredded by the time I step onto the dock at the Mykonos port. Achilles is there waiting and he sounds excited as he rushes over to greet me. For a moment, I'm speechless because I'm shocked at how short he is. We haven't seen each other for two weeks and I've forgotten his height is a lowly five foot six. He's short even for me, and I've gone out with numerous short men. Shouldn't I be meeting someone like the tall Australian who taught windsurfing at Atsitsa? Facing Achilles on the dock, while the other passengers rush down the gangplank, the answer comes: I don't have a set physical type. I'm drawn to iconoclasts, and a man like Achilles who is interesting to talk with is worth a thousand tall windsurfers.

For lunch, Achilles takes me to a popular bar. Hundreds of

delicate hand-blown glass lights in varying shades of blue or rose are hanging from the ceiling, the colours of a Mediterranean sunset. The lights are strikingly beautiful, without a doubt the most beautiful lights I've ever seen. Achilles explains that he made the lights I'm admiring and that his company sells his glass-blown artifacts to bars and restaurants all over the islands, and on the mainland of Greece too. Later, someone from Atsitsa will tell me that Achilles is one of the best-known glass-blowers in Greece. I'm too embarrassed to tell him how I stereotyped him as a shop-keeper selling tourist trinkets, although he would probably find my mistake hilarious.

He and I spend the day driving around Mykonos on his motorcycle; we have cappuccinos at Ftelia Beach, a favourite wind-surfing spot, and dinner at a restaurant on the twisting complex of cobblestone streets called Matoyianni that has made Mykonos famous. Afterwards, Achilles and I admire the sunset from the second-floor balcony of our small hotel by the port. The wind is soft and warm, and the stars are out while I sit thinking about our aborted attempt at sex a few minutes before. Achilles has brought a kit of beautiful Mediterranean sponges for us to use in the hotel bath, but his romantic idea turns into a farce when I'm too big to fit into the small Greek tub with him. What can you do? My body has a way of turning ordinary situations into a burlesque routine. Laughing, we decide to drink peach schnapps on the balcony instead. As we sit enjoying the evening, a Scandinavian tourist with ragged blond hair asks if he can join us. He's sobbing drunkenly, tears spilling from his eyes. Achilles motions for him to sit down. Looking grateful, the man throws himself on one of the deck chairs and weeps as he explains that he's just met his son whom he hasn't seen for fifteen years because he's divorced from the boy's mother. In an anguished voice, he says his son has rejected him.

There's a burst of maternal tsk-tsk noises as Achilles pulls his chair close to the stranger. He tenderly cups the man's face between his palms and says that life will bring the man's son his way again. The man stops crying and looks hopeful. I realize I'm holding my breath. Why is it surprising that Achilles would be kind to a stranger?

It occurs to me that despite my enlightening travels, I still see most men as unfeeling louts or self-absorbed children—shades of the superiority my mother felt about male immaturity.

There's no way around it. Most of my experiences in Greece seem to turn into lessons in accepting my own humanity along with the humanity of the people I meet.

Before we leave the next morning, I buy one of Achilles's small light blue vases from a shop by our hotel. I keep it on my desk as I write, a beautiful piece of hand-blown glass that reminds me not to make snap judgments about people, particularly people from a country whose cultural references I don't understand.

It's obvious North Americans like myself have a lot to learn from the Greeks, who don't care if they fail to look like movie stars. Their classical statues of the human body are unfailingly beautiful, but the statues are idealized forms, and most Greeks likely never resembled the stylized versions their artists created. Perhaps many Greek men in ancient times looked more like Achilles. In any case, the Greeks embrace with gusto the pleasures of the physical world that make up life in their country, and they believe they have every right to be there just as they are.

Meanwhile, Achilles and his story about the friend in Crete have started to take on extra meaning for me. Travelling is like breathing, I have Casanova say in the novel I later write about him. So exhale the old, inhale the new, and allow your heartbreak to fall away behind you . . . what you desire always awaits you if you are brave enough to recognize it.

3.

The first summers I spend in Greece I'm working on my novel *The Wives of Bath*. It tells the story of three rebellious boarding school girls in the early 1960s who loathe being girls and long to occupy the heroic roles that boys are encouraged to play. Its narrator, Mouse Bradford, admires her roommate, a girl named Paulie who wants to be a man. Mouse doesn't share Paulie's desire to change her gender but she wants to acquire masculine attributes, assuming that being like men will give her power.

The following June, I return to Athens to work on it for a month. Over the winter through an exchange of letters, Achilles has evolved from lover to friend, and he sounds pleased when he accepts my invitation to come for drinks at my apartment. As we sit tossing back small glasses of ouzo, he notices the row of Gothic novels on my bookshelf.

The novels, which include *Wuthering Heights* and *The Mysteries of Udolpho*, are part of the research I'm doing for my book.

Those paperbacks don't look like much fun! He laughs and lights up one of his endless cigarettes. The Gothic? He shakes his head. Not for me. I'm Greek.

He falls silent when I explain the novel was triggered by a true story from the 1970s about a Toronto girl named Susan Lynn Wood. Badly misunderstood and desperate to become the man she believed she was, she killed an elderly taxicab driver, cut his genitals off his dead body, and pasted them on herself. Susan Wood was found not guilty by reason of insanity, and she performed that cruel act of self-assertion during a time when there was little public understanding about gender dysphoria. Today she would receive counselling and likely drugs from medical practitioners, but that awareness was non-existent then. She committed the crime to prove to the father of her girlfriend that she was a man, and the act soon brought her to the attention of the authorities.

I'm writing a Gothic novel, I tell Achilles, because Gothic novels deal with repressed passion, and I point out that you don't need to go very far outside Athens to see Gothic superstition in some of the Greek villages.

He's no longer making jokes by the time I finish, although the skeptical look on his face suggests he isn't convinced.

And of course, he's correct about one thing: writing a Gothic tale is an odd thing to do while I'm enjoying a way of life that means relaxing into the rhythms of the day, feasting on fried calamari and retsina, and meeting new people.

However, I'm writing about a dark misunderstood crime and I know my Gothic novel will be a controversial book, so beneath the daily pleasures of life in Greece, I worry about the book's reception and the reaction of my readers.

This becomes clear in 1992 when I rent a small house in the village of Afionas, Corfu.

The White House

It's August 15, St. Spyridon's Day, a local holiday in Corfu that celebrates the island saint who was so virtuous his corpse smelled as sweet as roses. All the hotels are likely booked, but I'm taking my chances on finding a room and going up to Kalami to see Lawrence Durrell's White House. I don't have anything practical like a sleeping bag, so I may have to camp out on the beach in my jeans and green silk blouse and festival party hat. I'm taking along a glossy copy of Durrell's *The Greek Islands*. The shocking intimations of incest by his daughter in *Granta* (Autumn 1991) have lessened my interest in his work.

But I'm drawn to his non-fiction about Corfu because he once lived in a rented house in Kalami with his first wife, Nancy. It is there, in a building known as the White House, that he wrote *The Black Book*, his first well-received novel before *The Alexandria Quartet* made him famous in the late 1950s. *Prospero's Cell*, Durrell's non-fiction account of those Kalami days, describes him writing in a room overhung with cypress and olive trees.

I think of Durrell as my bus rumbles past college boys, their heads haloed by the roll bars of their Jeeps, and British tourists with sunburnt backs sitting under red-and-white Amstel umbrellas, drinking beer and eating pub snacks.

I get off the bus a few miles up the highway at a small sign that says *Kalami* and walk the half mile down the rolling hill, past overgrown villas and the cone-shaped cypress trees.

It's a long walk down the hill, and it's hot—*zeste*, the Greeks say—and the cove is very small, and the beach is shady at four o'clock in the afternoon. I need to find a room for the night, so I ask a group of young Italians on the road for directions, and they point me to the first taverna on the beach.

There are no rooms to rent in the taverna. Discouraged, I order an Amstel and sit beside an old Greek man at the bar. There's a commotion behind us. Heads turn. The seven Italians I met on the road have come in. Some wear Sony Walkman headsets, and all of them are short and noodle-thin with well-clipped hair. In Corfu, as in many parts of Greece, the young Italian men exude style. They travel in packs. They banter with each other like hyperactive children and cruise women in a swarm. Usually, there's no real threat—it's just the Mediterranean hustle. The Greeks are low-key, and the Italians are noisy, but they all come on to you.

The Italian boys walk over, smiling at me as if I were an old friend. A bad sign. The tallest one comes forward, shoving cigarettes and a beer my way. "Marlboros? Amstel? Pepsi? Ouzo?" As he stands there grinning, one of his friends steps up behind him and pours a beer over his head. The other young men shriek and call out words in Italian. He looks like he's going to weep. So I take one of his cigarettes because I feel sorry for him. (A mistake—done in by my Canadian manners.) He sits down beside me, the beer still dripping off his head. As he mops himself off with a napkin, I tell him I'm forty-six and have no interest in male company (an old alibi to get me off the hook). He smirks and orders a round of beers. His friends keep looking our way and shouting encouragement in screechy, insistent voices.

Scowling at them, I get up and leave. Outside, I hurry anxiously along the small road at the back of the beach, stopping at shabby-looking cottages and one or two small modern apartments. Nobody has rooms for the night.

Halfway up the hill, I hear high-pitched male voices. I turn around and see the young Italian men. "Marlboros? Amstel? Pepsi? Ouzo?" one of them shouts. The young man whose cigarette I took in the bar calls that they are going to make spaghetti for dinner, and they want me to come. I shake my head and continue up the hill towards the villas. They stand on the curve of the road below me like a flock of crows. Then I forget about them.

The sign at the front door says *COMPLETO*. I ring the bell anyway and there's no answer so I go back down the hill, and for the first time, I notice the sign in the olive grove that says tenting or camping is strictly forbidden by Law 392. The olive grove is out.

I turn in at a sign that says *The White House*. The top floor of Durrell's old home is rented; the bottom floor is a restaurant. I settle in with an Amstel on the large terrace overlooking the Kalami cove. A Greek army boat is inching its way across the strait to Albania, perhaps looking for Albanian refugees. They aren't wanted in Greece. There's smoke on the hills of Albania, and the young waiter George, who grew up in a nearby village, tells me the Albanians are burning the hillsides to grow new grass. I tell him I'm planning to sleep on the beach, and he says I shouldn't worry about Law 392. Nobody will report me. He shakes his head, frowning. But the mosquitoes. He sighs knowingly. It will be a little uncomfortable.

I'm in that no-man's-land of time in the Greek day—the hours before dinner gets underway around 9 p.m. I try to imagine Durrell and his first wife, Nancy, swimming like dolphins in the water just a few yards away. That's how Miller describes them in his travel book about Greece, *The Colossus of Maroussi*. Likely Miller slept in the room just above me, drinking Metaxa brandy and writing his letters of passion and enthusiasm—something he does even if he's in the same house with the people he's addressing. I feel a kinship because Miller, like me, has sometimes been maligned for writing about sex.

An hour passes. People slowly filter into the bar and terrace. It's dark outside now, and for the first time Durrell's presence is tangible. George the waiter shows me Durrell's portrait over the bar. The writer looks like any tousle-haired young man riding a motor scooter.

As I eat my dinner, stuffed vine leaves and prawns, a ghostly watery feeling takes me over, as if Durrell has left an aching sadness behind in this little seafaring cove. I stare morosely at the moonlit shadows behind the cypress trees. Only four miles away lurks the pale, hulking shape of Albania. It's a lost political kingdom, and Kalami is an oasis of literary longing.

Nostalgia pervades Corfu towns. The sadness of exile and failure lingers. The Romans, the Venetians, the Turks, and the British all tried to impose their ways on the Greeks, but nothing remains of their efforts except a few tourist ruins. The Greek culture endures because you can't change the Greeks—they change you. I look to Greece for a sense of connection to the ancient world, and in Corfu, I resent having to approach it layer by layer through the cultures that have come there before me. In Corfu, I feel foremost the atmosphere of those other seekers whose story, like Durrell's sadness, is waiting like a ghost on the stair. And yet when he was living here, Durrell wasn't famous. And the Second World War hadn't happened. So why should Durrell be sad at a time in his life when he's young and free?

It's 8:45 in the evening, and down at the beach, people are still swimming. That comforts me. Perhaps people will swim off and on all through the night, and I won't be alone with my band of Italians. And then I see them coming down the road to the White House. They head towards me full of energy from their spaghetti and walking as if they are bouncing on the road, bouncing right up in the air. Suddenly, I'm exhausted. They are heading my way, and I know that means trying to avoid them in the bar while the other tourists watch. George the waiter will help me dismiss them, but how can George fend them off during the night? They shriek louder and louder. People's heads turn in their direction. Any second now and they'll be here. I pick up my bag and leave quickly by the front entrance.

Rushing over, they alight around me like scavengers. One of them grabs my braids. I stand frozen. They are all shorter than I am, which is a bonus, but they have me surrounded. What should I do? Punch the one who grabbed me? Run? Screaming at them in Greek, George the waiter races down the steps and pulls me back up onto the terrace. They retreat. Inside the bar, George orders me a taxi and it comes in five minutes. A miracle. The driver was just coming down the coast when he heard the call. Afionas, I tell him, and he looks shocked until I assure him that I'm willing to pay the fifty bucks it will cost to take me the thirty miles of twisting road to the other side of the island. And then I thank George, who leads me out the back entrance, away from the Italians.

In the cab, I can't stop thinking about the Italian boys and what they might have done. Would their playfulness have turned ugly if I didn't do what they wanted? If I had slept on the beach, would they have tried to rape me, or simply kept on pestering me? The question is unsettling. A woman is particularly vulnerable in a situation like the one I've just experienced. And even though I'm used to fighting back I wouldn't be strong enough to hold off a group of young athletic men determined to assault me. There's no use wondering. I'll never know what might have happened, because my taxi is speeding up the bluffs under Corfu's largest mountain, the Pantokrator. We're passing mountain villages where Greeks are celebrating their fragrant St. Spyridon. Just before midnight, the taxi stops in my own village square.

I pay the driver and walk through the silent streets of the small village and up the cliff to see the moon from the vantage point of the donkey parking lot. (The field at the top of the cliff behind Afionas is where the farmers tether their donkeys for the night.) Does my vista compare to Durrell's? I stand for a long time, staring at the grand bay of Agios Georgios and the stern limestone bluffs whose sparse growth of olive trees resembles a male face with a five o'clock shadow. Of course my view compares. In Greece, every man and every woman is a proud citizen of their own village.

Looking back, I understand Durrell's sadness. It is so obvious I wonder why I didn't see it before, considering what I was doing. Durrell had gone to Corfu to write books, and like me, he was on his third novel, *The Black Book*, writing with urgency and some desperation. It's the first novel of his that will win critical praise, but he doesn't know that back in 1936 when he writes about it in a letter to his friend Alan G. Thomas. In a book of his essays and letters, *Spirit of Place*, Durrell writes: "I've been very down in the jaw lately over this fucking book [*The Black Book*], which won't go as it should. It's difficult. If I ever finish it to my satisfaction, I shall feel that virtue has gone out of me. Real virtue. It's like fine crochet. . . . Very queer and difficult for an up and down chap like me."

Before I visited Durrell's White House, my aloneness in Afionas was beginning to get to me. I would wake up anxious about my novel. I wrote in my journal: *Not sure the hunched shoulder that my narrator calls Alice works as a device for my narrator telling her story.* There are dozens of pages like this one, paragraph after paragraph of a writer's fret over one problem or another.

How could I miss the source of Durrell's despair—the ghostly sadness I sensed at his White House? It had nothing to do with Corfu, or his wrecked marriages, or the disgrace to come after the allegation of incest with his daughter.

It's obvious that he and I were experiencing the agony of a writer working on a sexually provocative novel, wondering if the critics will like it—if anybody will like it—and knowing the book is an important test. This isn't as true now, but the taint of disapproval still follows a writer (especially a woman writer) if they write about sex. Durrell was only twenty-four during that summer in Kalami, about the same age as the young Italians I've met in Corfu. What I felt then is an emotion as old as Greece itself: the writer's terror that their work won't be understood.

Like it or lump it, the body is our portal

1.

My daughter, Sam, sits beside me in the taxi from Mitilini giddy with excitement as we speed up and down and over the round, wooded mountains of Lesbos, passing through nameless villages, some with therapeutic hot springs, and traversing small plains and olive groves that must've been there since the days of Homer. Lesbos, with the exception of its western side, is almost subtropically green and lush. Some tourist guides claim it has more sunshine than other parts of Greece, more sunshine even than any other part of the Mediterranean. The Roman historian Tacitus said its climate is noble and agreeable. I'm in Lesbos for July, and my daughter has joined me for a workshop, something we both need.

My life has changed radically since the early nineties, although I'm still writing novels and teaching. My daughter has just moved into the apartment below the one I share with Patrick in the Toronto duplex we have rented. For most of her teenage years, she's lived with her father, and even though we continued to spend holidays and many weekends together, our relationship needs attention. She's an adult now, trying to figure out how to make her way in the world as a young woman, and I'm determined to set aside the time to help her with her struggles. Over the winter, she had fallen into a depression and dropped out of McGill University, my alma mater, to take a gap year. She said she was unhappy with college life.

A psychologist told me once that boys act out immediately when their parents divorce while girls don't express their anger until they're in their twenties. That day in the taxi, Sam is twenty-four, and she's angry with me about her childhood. My divorce from her father meant she grew up in a polarized situation where my left-leaning liberal values clashed with her father's more conservative business approach. Angry may be too mild a word. Rage is more like it. She was furious with me for leaving her father and for the difficulties she experienced growing up as a child of divorced parents. She found our arguments over her childcare exhausting and painful and she disliked going back and forth between our houses. One afternoon while Patrick watched in amazement, she yelled at the top of her voice that I had failed her as a mother. She told me I hadn't been there enough for her when she was growing up and that it was too late now for me to step in and mother her. She said I needed to back off and that she was old enough to make her own decisions. It was an awful experience, and yet it felt familiar because I'd done the same thing at her age.

Sometimes the quickest way to assert our independence from our mothers is to blame them for our problems while hoping they'll still love and approve of us. When I was twenty, I blasted my mother for choosing a marriage with security and comfort instead of following her desire to write books. I told her I wasn't going to have a bourgeois life like hers because I wanted my face to look as if I had really lived. I don't think she ever forgave me for that cruel (and unnecessary) comment, although all I really wanted was for her to say she would still love me if I chose a different path.

I didn't want my daughter's attempt to separate to end the same way. So I kept my mouth shut and listened. Besides, Sam had a point: my marriage had been a youthful mistake, and she paid the price for it just as I did.

Things have become less tense since Sam blew up at me and she seems pleased to be spending a few weeks in July in Lesbos, so I feel encouraged. I've started spending part of my summers on the island because the late feminist theologian Carol Christ has a house in Molivos, and she's helping me with a novel about women and their spiritual quests. Carol is part of the large group of American feminists and women scholars who started the goddess movement during the 1970s.

I tell my daughter that Carol has a PhD in religious studies from Yale University but her feminist views on religion mean she can't get a tenured teaching job at a major American university. Christian professors run the programs, and they see her scholarship as outside the academic mainstream. So she moved to Greece and founded the Ariadne Institute for the Study of Myth and Ritual. Her institute conducts workshops in Lesbos and tours of Minoan shrines in Crete, and I've enrolled my daughter and myself in one of these workshops, which are a zesty mix of Carol's knowledge of religious myths and history; Sappho's poems; some beautiful re-created rituals based on the Minoans; and a great deal of hearty Greek cooking.

As we pass the vast, marshy inlet of Kalloni, my daughter stops looking at the view and asks me to tell her about my friend. Why do I think Carol's workshop will help someone like her?

I explain that I'm hoping she will get some insights that will help her understand who she is and what she wants out of life. I think, but don't say: I hope her journey towards self-acceptance and a community that appreciates her won't be as hard as mine, and if she can draw from any wisdom I have found on my travels, so much the better. I don't expect her to become a carbon copy of me. I hope instead that she will find a way to use what I've learned in order to become her own person. Maybe that's the prayer of every loving parent.

I assure her that she will meet young women her age at the workshop as well as their mothers and grandmothers, along with women without children. They will be coming to Lesbos like us, bringing their personal problems and any spiritual questions they have about women's relationship to traditional religions.

I point out that religion in Western culture, with the exception of the Virgin Mary, has ignored the selfhood of women, and Carol has given me a framework for my spiritual views that I couldn't find anywhere else. My daughter looks interested, and I consider explaining how unfair it is that feminist scholars like Carol are regularly accused of substituting a female deity for a male God when they're interested in expanding the rituals and liturgies of traditional religious practices to include women. When God is a man, man is God, Mary Daly, another feminist theologian, once said. She could have added: When only heterosexual men can be God, it's harder for everyone else to see their reflection in the spiritual dimension.

The criticism of Carol is especially misleading since she believed that everyone, no matter who they are, represents the divine. As she grew older, she became interested in process philosophy, which had been started by Alfred Whitehead, and she was struck by the work of Charles Hartshorne, one of Whitehead's followers, who believed that birds sing not only to establish territory and find mates but because they enjoy singing. Hartshorne, like Carol, believed our bodies bind us to the physical processes of life, so we need to learn how to enjoy the experience of being alive. It's a view that sits comfortably with my own.

But it's never wise to talk up your spiritual philosophy, in case it's conflated with proselytizing, and it's better if my daughter is free to discover those aspects on her own. I need to choose my words carefully, so I say, Would you like to hear about my experiences in Minoan Crete? They were wild. She smiles and nods and that's all the encouragement I need.

2.

As I start my story, Sam and I are heading up the back end of Mount Lepetymnos, the side that faces away from the Turkish coast.

In September 1995, I tell my daughter, I took a tour of Minoan Crete with Carol Christ, and I caught a bad cold on the plane coming over, so I can't stop blowing my nose and coughing as I stand waiting for our tour group to assemble in our hotel in downtown Heraklion. Heraklion is the capital of the island, with a population of over two hundred thousand people in the city and surrounding area.

I'm not prepared for the first sight of Carol Christ, I explain, but there's no question that's who is walking towards me in the lobby, because she has written about her height. This big woman who calls herself Karolina, Greek for Carol, is extraordinarily tall with a fully curvaceous body, long blond hair, and the dainty face of an old-fashioned female doll.

She is dressed in soft, flowing clothes that I'll always associate with her. An assortment of gold rings and gold bracelets shine on her fingers and wrists, and she has draped an elegant, feminine scarf about her shoulders. She could be a heroine in a girls' school movie, the fierce Amazonian teacher who protects her students from an unfeeling headmistress.

However, before I met her, I found it hard to believe that another woman could be as tall as me. So I find myself staring, amazed as she strides purposefully towards me and our group of twenty tourist women who stand waiting by the tour bus.

We look each other in the eye warily. Neither of us has met a woman our size before, and we're nervous. Are we going to be friends? When you meet your doppelgänger comparisons can pop up, and comparisons usually bring feelings of rivalry.

Before the tour, Carol had written to me that she felt unsure about a professional writer joining one of her tours. Would I come as a cynic and naysayer? What if I wrote a negative review of her Minoan pilgrimage? Journalists sometimes portrayed women like her as flakes despite the years of academic study that she had done.

In my reply, I did my best to reassure Carol. I felt a kinship with this woman whose large female body must have been the triggering impulse behind her religious philosophy, just as my own body was for me and my fiction writing. It's that outsider perspective again; it can lead to the creation of a new way of looking at things, which Carol has accomplished in her feminist scholarship.

That afternoon in the hotel lobby, she takes a quick, startled look at the dirty jeans and well-worn T-shirt I've put on, thinking they would be the right outfit for scrambling over archaeological ruins. But it turns out we aren't going to rugged sites in the country that afternoon. A few years later, she'll send me an email about what meeting me for the first time meant to her:

Though I know that I am a head taller than many of my friends, I literally have no idea how I look in the world because there is no one to whom I can compare myself. Since almost everyone else sees someone who is about their height, weight, and coloring every day, it is hard for others to imagine how strange it makes you feel not ever to see anyone who looks like you. I was just about to turn fifty when I met you. Meeting you helped me to overcome a lifetime of feeling I was different from everyone else.

I understood what she was talking about. It's the same thing Michelle Obama said in her memoir, *The Light We Carry*. When you don't see other people who look like you, you can't form a mental picture of yourself.

Being tall has been somewhat different for my daughter, due to the emergence of supermodels and the list of quips she used to keep handy for anyone who tried to put her down about her height. But neither Carol nor I had been told what to say back when people mocked our size, and that morning in Heraklion, she doesn't comment on my height like most people do when they meet me for the first time. She was obviously avoiding the usual clichéd comments like, How's the weather up there? or Do you play basketball? Instead, Carol shakes my hand formally and welcomes our group before she introduces Andreas, our Greek bus driver. A few minutes later, we climb on board our tour bus. On this first day of our tour, we're heading for the ancient Minoan ruins of Knossos. The archaeological site has been called the oldest capital in Europe. It's in the Greek countryside on the north coast of Crete about five kilometres from Heraklion, and the palace whose ruins cover over two hundred acres is remarkable for the beauty of its design and for its lack of military defences.

At Knossos, we file down the processional pathway to the Central Court with its view of the wall murals and two-storey terra cotta columns of lime plaster. Nearby is the Hall of the Double Axes, the symbol that Carol says represents the creative power of the great Minoan earth mother. The Central Court is filled with tourists looking at their guidebooks, and as we stand listening to Carol, I hear a woman say to her husband, You see, dear, there was a time when women ruled the earth. The man looks startled and then bemused, as if the prospect of women ruling anything is too silly to consider. Whether intentionally or not, Carol is providing a context to their conversation, because suddenly, she's talking loudly about matriarchal Neolithic cultures, which she says were egalitarian. She points out that these societies were not an upside-down version of our male-dominated Western societies, and there's no archaeological evidence that they suppressed the rights of men.

There are pleased, surprised noises from our group, which is made up mostly of American women, whose ages range from twenty-five to seventy. Carol and I, who are both fifty, are somewhere in the middle.

She nods, smiling at the tourists carrying guidebooks and says we shouldn't pay attention to tourist information that claim Minoan Crete was ruled by a king and that it didn't need military fortifications because it had a strong navy. According to Carol, the guidebooks were influenced by the work of Arthur Evans, the British archaeologist who excavated Knossos in the early twentieth century. Evans, who restored a large part of the site, named Minoan Crete after King Minos, even though the real King Minos lived long after the end of Minoan culture. Instead, Carol says Minoan Crete, with its ruined palaces and towns, was a culture that worshipped a Bronze Age goddess.

As she talks, I realize the site of Knossos is a battleground between the traditional ideas of male archaeologists, who see kings and armies in ancient ruins, and feminist archaeologists like the late Marija Gimbutas, a Lithuanian American who compiled a detailed inventory of over two thousand Bronze Age artifacts that she found in Greece and other places. In his introduction to her book, *The Language of the Goddess*, Joseph Campbell compared Gimbutas's inventory to the work of French scholar Jean-François Champollion, who deciphered the Rosetta stone.

Like Gimbutas, Carol believes that the designs of spirals, snakes, chevrons, and triangles in the Neolithic artifacts are a pictorial language that describes the mystery of transformation. She says the small clay figurines of the goddesses found in the Neolithic ruins in Europe represent the metaphysical power of the universe at its deepest level; they were not fertility goddesses or wives of male gods, as many male archaeologists claim.

On the way out of Knossos, I don't find any scenes on the palace walls of military triumphs or women serving the kinglike figures, although I have made it my business to keep an eye out. Nor do I find images glorifying war or the taking of booty, or showing the processions of slaves, or honouring kings—or anything else that would lead me to think she was mistaken.

From Knossos, the tour bus drives us to the nearby Heraklion Archaeological Museum with its numerous Minoan exhibits. Judging from the displays of pottery and murals, with their enchanting images of dark-haired snake goddesses, the Minoans appear to have lived in a thriving artistic culture whose art bears no relation to the warlike imagery common in our Western societies.

At this point in our taxi ride, my daughter interrupts my impassioned explanation and asks if I can stop talking about archaeologists like Gimbutas and tell her what happened on my trip in Crete. Nodding my head, I think: *Gimbutas is one of the great archaeologists of our time and she's been overlooked. You should know about her.* But I don't say that, I say, Of course, and finish my account of the first day.

At a shop near Knossos, I buy a glass charm called the blue eye and stick it in my purse. Carol sees what I'm doing and says in Greece a blue eye is always pinned to the clothing of a baby when it is taken outside the house. She suggests it will be a good thing to put on the altar the following day when we visit the cave at Skoteino. I don't understand what she's talking about, and the idea of descending into the earth unnerves me. Ever since I was a child I've been afraid of heights, and going deep underground brings up the same fears.

3.

I've been dreading the descent into the Skoteino cave all morning, I tell my daughter. But it's what I signed up for and Carol says our group will enjoy the spiritual experience of reliving the way many Minoans worshipped their goddesses. (*Skoteino* means "dark" in Greek.)

The cave goes down to a depth of more than 150 feet and has four separate levels. I'm not sure if I can handle the descent, especially since I still feel tired and listless from my cold, but I don't mention my nervousness to anyone, and for luck, I bring along the blue glass eye I bought from the tourist shop near Knossos.

The first level of the cave is an enormous room surrounded by lumpy rock formations. The second level turns out to be a smaller room with an alcove that shelters a tall stalagmite. Carol identifies the formation as the Minoan goddess Vritomartis, sometimes known as the goddess of mountains and hunting. *So far, so good.* I finger the blue good luck charm in my pocket nervously as the women place lit candles and small goddess figurines around the makeshift altar. Others add stones or jewellery while Carol pours milk and honey on their offerings and then wine and water.

I'm touched by the solemnity of the occasion, and the eerie beauty of the amber beams of the women's flashlights wandering across the cave walls, which are sweating like ripe cheese. The flashlights illuminate small, carved animals in the walls. Some of the large stalactites that hang from the cave ceiling have merged with the stalagmite formations rising from the cave floor. The visual effect of the strange moist formations is like staring at the intestines of an unearthly prehistoric creature.

Next to the altar is a small hole in which Minoans had dropped their offerings. Carol and some of the women throw down small objects like worry beads or olives before we continue downward.

Spelunking to the third level is a piece of cake, but the descent to the fourth level is strenuous. We've been underground for only thirty minutes and already I feel exhausted. There's an unpleasant tickle in my throat. *Remember you can always turn back*, I tell myself, although the passageway ahead is getting narrower, so turning back will soon be impossible, especially with the long line of women coming up behind me. As I shuffle forward, steeling myself, the tickle grows worse and I begin to cough uncontrollably. The barking sound is embarrassingly loud in the darkness of the cave, and hysterical thoughts bubble up inside me. What on earth was I thinking? Carol may have led some successful expeditions into the cave, but even with our experienced Greek guides, how do any of us know it's really safe? If one of the passageways collapses we'll be trapped inside the earth. My large body isn't suited for such a narrow claustrophobic space. Behind me, I can hear two women talking about going back. Fighting down my feelings of shame, I turn to join them. There's a sudden rustling noise behind me and somebody shines a flashlight on my feet. Don't move, a woman's voice whispers.

I look down. We're standing on a steep cliff face. Women are lined up in front of me and behind me, and their bodies are blocking the way in both directions. Turning back is out of the question. I begin to cough again. My invisible helper puts a Loutraki bottle in my hand. I drink the water greedily, and my coughing stops. Whispering encouragement, she shines her light on the guide standing ahead of us on the ledge. He has positioned his body so that his hands are touching the cave wall, and women are walking under his arms and out the other side. He's protecting them from falling. Beyond these women, others are edging through a human-sized hole in the stone, moving tentatively, taking their time. I can feel myself tremble, and my breathing starts coming in rushing gulps.

My helper taps my shoulder. Breathe slowly, she hisses. I do what she says and my breathing gradually slows. Soon I'm calm enough to walk under the guide's arms. I move carefully, trying not to think about falling. Ahead, a small group of women are waiting in front of the hole in the cave wall. I stand and wait too, averting my eyes from the fathomless black depth beyond the ledge. When my turn comes, I manage to crawl through the opening.

On the other side, I find myself in a small passageway, about the length and width of two staircases. Sitting on my haunches, trembling with relief, I half slide, half crawl to what looks like a large oval room with high ceilings.

We stand in almost total darkness. A few of the women's flash-lights are once again weaving across the cave walls, and lighting up a tall reddish stalagmite rising out of the cave floor. Carol says it could be an image of the goddess and suggests we sit around it. We do what she says, and I purposefully sit close to my helper, who turns out to be Jana Ruble, the petite red-haired woman who helps Carol with her Minoan pilgrimages. Jana had been the one, not me, to stay cool-headed, and her sangfroid reminds me of stories of short men having an advantage in military battles because their centre of gravity is lower to the ground.

The group lights candles and places them at the feet of the stalagmite. After a few minutes of silence, Carol begins to speak. She suggests we say our names and the names of our mothers and grandmothers and great-grandmothers, as far back as we can remember.

I hear my voice call out: I am Susan, daughter of Jane, grand-daughter of Pauline, great-granddaughter of Daisy. And then I stop. I don't know the names of my other female ancestors. Link-ing myself to them in the darkness of the cave feels strange, and

I'm surprised to discover I can go back only a few generations. None of the other women can either. They call out one or two names of their female ancestors and then stop. How extraordinary that we have to get to the bottom of a cave in Crete to discover we don't know our female lineage.

It's time for more offerings, Carol says in a hushed voice. I fish in my pocket for my Greek good luck charm and place it on the altar. It's helped keep me safe, after all.

4.

Back in Heraklion that evening, I buy Jana, my helper in the cave, a jug of retsina as our group of women gorge on local food at a nearby taverna. Some women read out their favourite poems by Sappho while others exchange stories about their mothers. Carol reads a passage from her book *Odyssey with the Goddess*, in which she says that our relationships with our mothers are often tinged with pain because they raised us in a culture that doesn't value women. They didn't receive the support they needed, and sometimes they didn't give us that support either.

I start to tell Carol that mothers who are unfair to their children don't just act as a result of political repression, although such repression doesn't help. Then I stop myself. I'll probably always be skeptical of the view that egalitarian matriarchal societies were as peaceful as Carol describes because it seems too easy to project onto Neolithic cultures the longing for characteristics our own culture lacks. But nobody really knows, and it's possible I'm wrong.

The Cretan waiter brings us platters of crusty red-brown mullet, barbounia, and side plates of tiny Cretan olives, along with paximadia, the sour local bread that needs to be moistened in water. Toasting me with a glass of raki, the Cretan moonshine, she asks what I think of the tour.

It's an eye-opener, I reply. And Carol nods when I add how hard it is to imagine an ancient culture with different values from our own.

As she finishes her coffee, I tell her the story of how my mother expected me to live with her and be her emotional companion after my father died.

In the taxi, my daughter looks surprised, and I explain that I don't usually talk about this time in my life with anyone so it's a relief to be able to describe the intense way my mother leaned on me at a time when I was desperate to be living an adventurous life as a writer. Neither my mother nor anyone one else in the family seemed to notice the sacrifice she was asking of me, and I kept my feelings to myself. As a child, I felt responsible for my mother. I've had that feeling ever since I was small: I needed to protect her because my father wasn't paying attention. Then he died and she was overwhelmed by shock and grief.

You had to be strong, Carol replies. Or you and your mother would have been washed away in a sea of tears. It was a lot of pressure on you.

I tell Carol that I have a tendency to jump in and help people in a crisis, without asking if they want my help, and in my case the feeling is probably linked to the fact that I am big, so I think I should pick up the extra load. *Big, big, big.* My size seeps into everything.

My equation goes like this: *You're big so you have the biggest responsibility. People and their silly aggressions can't hurt someone as tall and powerful as you.* It was true of my father, and the years I spent growing up in his house led me to think it was true of me too: we saw ourselves as giants, and somewhere along the way we both began to believe in the myth of our invincibility.

Carol smiles. Intimacy is based on sharing feelings of vulnerability, she says. It's hard to feel close with people if we don't.

Of course, she's right. It's the same thing with novels. Unless writers show readers the vulnerability of their characters, they'll churn out wooden prose.

Carol wonders if my father's habit of overestimating his strength eventually cost him his life. I tell her it did. He was consumed by his self-image as a strong, giant-like healer. My guess is he wanted to avoid looking weak. And I'm frightened of looking weak too. Am I just copying my father? I ask Carol.

She says that's up to me to figure out.

Before I left for Crete in 1995, I had a powerful dream about two snakes jumping in and out of the giant clay jars called pithoi, which the Minoans used for storing grain and olive oil. One snake was skinny and small and slow while the other snake was big and muscular. It moved at lightning speed, jumping back and forth from one jar to the other.

When my talk with Carol is over, I rush back to my hotel room to use the technique for analyzing dreams that I learned in Atsitsa. After our afternoon in the cave, the moment feels right. When I sit down to do the question-and-answer technique I hear noises outside my window. I put down my pen to listen. On the street outside, the birds are twittering in the leafy trees that line the boulevard by my hotel. The comforting sound tells me night is falling, and the fact that I can hear it in a city like Heraklion says everything about Greece and the way its connection to nature is more tangible and direct than in most big metropolitan areas.

When I pick up my pen again, I already know the answer to my dream's meaning: the skinny snake represents the doubtful, timid part of me doing its best to keep up with the big muscular python, which is the more determined and ambitious side of myself. My experience in the Minoan cave made it clear how uncomfortable I am with feeling vulnerable. If only I could slow down and show more compassion for the skinny slower snake trying so hard to catch up, how much easier and more enjoyable life would be.

5.

My daughter is still listening intently, and I wonder if I should tell her about my vision at the Minoan palace in Zakros. It's something I keep to myself because it's so easily misunderstood. I saw my vision at an abandoned shrine that stands on one of three hills near the Zakros Mountains. There's a spooky wildness about the mountains of Crete, something savage and unbowed, as if the setting has the power to draw you back across centuries to where the mists of ancient days will drift and swirl in surprising ways. Well why not? I'm on a roll with my storytelling, so there's no reason not to describe my mystical experience.

My cold, now in its final stages, has worn me down, I tell my daughter. I feel exhausted by the constant togetherness of the women and by the intense physical effort involved in visiting the ruins and caves. When we get off the tour bus, the group gathers around Carol, who is waiting for us in what remains of the ancient palace. Just as they were at Knossos, the buildings are made from blocks of limestone and plaster. They surround a stone courtyard that is approached along the stone pathways used by the religious initiates at the shrine. As the women get ready to leave their offerings of vegetables on the ancient altar, I let Carol know I feel worn out and sick and I need to go back to the bus and sleep. In a spirit of fun, I walk off down one of the processional paths, holding up my arms in the same gesture as a Minoan priestess, elbows bent, palms out, a posture intended to send out healing energy to the world.

Look! She's a snake goddess, one of the women jokes. Everyone laughs. I turn around and see an extraordinary sight: a small bright orange fire is burning in front of each woman's chest. The Greek sky is vast and blue behind them and there is not a single modern thing in my sight. Only the women with the tongues of radiant flames suspended in the air near their bodies while I stand on the Zakros hilltop, my mouth open as snot drips from my nose, my throat itchy and sore from coughing, a heavy fatigue weighing my body down.

What is going on? Am I really seeing what I'm seeing? Well, yes, I am, because there, about twenty feet away, the nineteen women are still staring at me while the flames are glowing like tiny lights in front of their chests. Something miraculous and eternal is happening, and for over a minute, as we stand gazing at one another, their ghostly fires flickering and glimmering, I see the tiny fires in front of each of their bodies as clearly as I see the rocky Cretan hillside, and a voice in my head says, *Keep still, and wait*, but I'm too overwhelmed to move anyway.

It's sometimes thought that a spiritual vision is a loud and ear-shattering experience of seeing the heavens crack open as a giant hand reaches down from the clouds to bless you. But what I'm seeing feels quiet and matter-of-fact.

Then my vision fades. One of the women points at a carving near the ancient pathway and they start talking to each other again, so I walk slowly back to the bus, aware that I have just experienced something that a religious person might describe as a moment of spiritual grace.

Curled up on a seat in the bus trying to sleep, it comes to me that although I'm no longer a practising Christian, what I saw is right out of my old Anglican Sunday school lesson about tongues of fire burning near the chests of Jesus's disciples gathered at a house in Jerusalem.

Did the religious education I received as a child cue me for a sight like this? Or is my vision a throwback to civilizations older than the Bible? I have no way of proving what I saw.

My daughter presses me to tell her what I think, and I say it was real enough but I don't know how to explain it. I add that I have no doubt that it happened to me, and possibly my confidence about what I experienced is the same thing an early group of Christians, the Gnostics, called a sense of knowing. The Gnostics believed spiritual experiences have little to do with faith or belief. Or logic. When Carl Jung was asked if he believed in God, he said he didn't *believe* in God; he knew God. He didn't need to convince others about what he knew. It was enough that he knew what he felt.

When I tell Carol later about what I saw, she isn't surprised.

She's seen visions while visiting some of the Minoan ruins, and so have numerous women on other tours. She thinks that under the right circumstances, spiritual energy can appear as a visual manifestation of the life force. At Yale, Carol used to tell her professors in religious studies that the authors of the Old Testament believed they were telling the truth when they described the trees and the hills singing. According to Carol, ancient people may literally have seen spiritual energy in the rocks and trees.

She says my vision of the flames burning in front of the women is part of a non-rational way of understanding spirituality. In Carol's theology, the human body is the ground of being, the place from which insights and wisdom flow. The opposite is true for Christian religion, with its focus on heaven, because Christianity emphasizes the relief of escaping the physical body. And possibly, that's one reason why so many of our Western technologies, including cellphones and computer screens, are designed to encourage us to leave our physical selves behind and participate more fully in a virtual world than a physical one.

However, Carol was telling me something I'd never considered before: she was telling me that our physical selves are the portals to spiritual truth. According to her, we become spiritual by thinking through our bodies, and our embodied way of thinking allows us to connect more deeply not only with ourselves but with other people too. Boxes, boxes everywhere, I wrote at the start of my story about the way my size has shaped my life. And of course, I knew instinctively, without Carol pointing it out, that our bodies are boxes too, the flesh-and-bone vessels that carry our spirits forward to the end of our lives. So why try to escape your body? Doesn't it make more sense to do what Carol suggests and inhabit it?

6.

Sam's attention is starting to drift, and I hesitate, wondering if I'm sounding like a preachy ideologue.

I ask myself: Are you being preachy?

Maybe.

Do you care?

Of course I care. But the struggle has always been there for all of us whose body doesn't fit gender norms.

Isn't that a fancy way of saying the obvious?

You mean it sucks to have a female body?

I wouldn't go that far. Besides, the most radical part of Carol's theology isn't about Neolithic societies worshipping a female deity. It's embodied spirituality.

What's embodied spirituality?

The knowledge that spiritual wisdom comes through the body.

Come again?

It means the body is the portal to understanding ourselves.

A portal to what?

To comprehending our link to the cosmos.

Don't give me that woo-woo goddess stuff. What would a society based on embodied spirituality look like?

It would be a calm, empathetic society without wars.

That will never happen.

It may have happened in Minoan Crete. And if it did, who says it can't happen again?

7.

Our taxi starts its winding descent down the switchbacks along Mount Lepetymnos, and I start worrying that I may be giving Sam the wrong impression. Should I double back and tell her how I really feel about myself? After all, don't I enjoy the experience of being a woman? Have I forgotten what happened to me when I dressed in male drag? After *The Wives of Bath* was published, offers to give talks come flooding in. For one lecture, I dressed up as a man because that novel describes, among other things, the plight of a girl who self-identifies as male. Before my talk, Janice, a young woman who specializes in male drag, helps me disguise myself. She feels safer dressed as a man because she is short and slight, and when she's in drag, men don't harass her. With quick deft strokes, she pencils in a mustache and some stubble and tucks my hair under a fedora. I rent a men's business suit from a costume shop and I set off as, wonder of wonders, a tall man.

As I go out the door, my convincing appearance horrifies my partner, Patrick. He says his entire psychosexual life with me just collapsed before his eyes. In his mind, I am a tall, beautiful woman, and suddenly I'm not. And how I look isn't what he signed up for. He gets it, but it freaks him out. I don't have time to unpack this with him because I need to drive up to the university. But I'm not worried. When I get back home I'll take off my costume and become myself again. I push away his unsettling reaction and hurry out the door. When I arrive at the university, without thinking what I'm doing I enter the women's bathroom. A cleaning woman is mopping the floor. She stops mopping and screams.

No, no! I try to reassure her. You're perfectly safe. I'm a woman. Her eyes wide in fear, she pushes past me carrying her mop. I follow her, trying to explain, and her screams grow louder. The terrified look on her face shocks me.

Janice, my drag king helper, has done her job too well. There is nothing I can say to reassure the cleaning woman.

Shaken by what has occurred, I rush off to give my lecture. The room is packed and several women academics who don't know I'm in drag are sitting in the front row. As I talk, I notice a change coming over them. They smile up at me flirtatiously, whispering among themselves and giggling. They don't seem like dignified professors. They seem like giddy schoolgirls responding to the cues of my masculine attire.

Stop being silly, I want to tell them. Look more closely and you'll see I'm really a woman. They keep tittering, and direct coy, covert looks at me. It's comical.

After the talk, a group of us go to a campus bar for a drink. I'm still in my fancy business suit and fedora, and I worry I won't be allowed in because of my get-up.

At the door, the grim face of the bouncer lights up as he extends his hand. Put it there, buddy, he says.

Instead of being pleased that I've fooled him, I feel as horrified as Patrick was a few hours before. My identity as a woman has been obliterated. Where is the real me in my clever drag costume? It seems I've stepped into the box of traditional masculinity, and

I feel trapped and uncomfortable. For the first time, I understand what the heterosexual men I know experience. Unless they are determined to fight these restrictions, they have less choice in how they look: they have to look manly. They have less choice in the way they express themselves: they have to sound manly. They have little choice about following the strict social code of the male box about what masculine means. They have to follow its rules: they can't do allegedly feminine things. They can't schlep around in sandals (although some men do). They can't put their hands on their hips. Really? Really. Let me know when you notice one of them doing it. They can't wear the colour pink. Many of them have been taught it's a show of weakness to apologize, and only a decade or two ago, they couldn't order quiche in a restaurant without someone making a wisecrack about their masculinity.

In my male get-up, I'm like someone experiencing the feeling of discomfort that comes if your gender identity differs from the sex assigned at birth. Because back rushed my old fears about not being feminine enough. Maybe I wasn't.

Well okay, the world seems to be saying, as a woman, you can present yourself as old-style fem, or you can act like guys who are blunt and direct. But if you were truly womanly, would people have been fooled so easily? Obviously, you have no trouble passing as a man. So who are you anyway? Are you a knock-off of Tiresias, the blind prophet who was transformed into a woman for seven years? Or are you non-binary, like numerous people these days?

When I meet Janice, my drag king helper, the next day, I tell her I'm not sure I want to dress in male drag again. She shrugs and smiles and I find myself shrugging and smiling too. I've made it out of the traditional male box in one piece. For me, it's a box without problems, because I can step in and out of it without getting stuck. But now that I know what heterosexual men experience, why would I go back to something that confining and regimented? Unless I get paid to do it. And even then.

8.

My daughter is starting to look impatient. I've been far away in my thoughts, and it's time to get out of my head. I have easier stories to understand than the one about my vision in Zakros. For example, why not describe what happened to me at a hot springs in Lesbos?

This experience took place a few weeks before you joined me in Lesbos, I tell Sam, and she nods, encouraging me to go on.

When Carol stops the car I'm sure she has taken me to the wrong spot because the springs are nothing to look at. They lie in the middle of a large grouping of misshapen rocks by the side of a poorly travelled road near the Mediterranean. You might drive by the location without noticing anything unless Carol is with you to point out the springs and the large oak tree nearby. Dangling from its branches are hundreds of small offerings— scarves, necklaces, and ribbons, even women's shoes and a pair of baby booties, probably left behind by someone hoping for a child. Just a few feet away, a dozen women are laughing and talking and some are spraying water at each other as they bathe in the thermal springs.

Standing there, watching the women inside the bubbling water, I think of the day I buried my shameful body in the sand by the polliwog pond. I remember how trapped and hopeless I felt to be stuck with my physical self. There was nothing I could do about my size except to hope I wouldn't grow more. And now, frolicking in the waters of the spa, are these women—some old, some young, some with bulky, shapeless bodies, some skinny, some with beautiful shiny hair, many with gleeful smiles—cavorting together as if they were children, enjoying who they are, giving themselves over to pleasure, and not caring one iota what I think of them. The older women with their baggy arms and wrinkled faces seem particularly carefree, as if they don't fear aging because, as I've discovered, they have other sources of power besides their physical appearance. They are old but so what, they seem to be saying. I keep staring at the women, and to my surprise, I'm not looking at their naked bodies the way I might at home, scrutinizing them for physical flaws. For a moment, my eyes are seeing the women without judgment. I'm looking at them in the same accepting way I might look at a pleasing garden or a grove of olive trees.

It seems as if I have travelled a great distance through time and experience to meet up with them. I know how lucky we are to have our bodies, to be alive in a world that despite its horrors has started to offer more room to be a woman. My writing, my relationships, my teaching, and my travels—all of it has been my way of proving that a woman like myself has a right to take up space. And my old mantra—to be tall is to be too big—is getting fainter and fainter as I take off my clothes and get in the water to join them.

I turn to my daughter to hear what she thinks of my story but she is no longer listening. She's looking eagerly out the window because our taxi has started climbing the Molivos hill to the large stone house where Carol stands waiting to greet us. The Mediterranean is a wash of pale blue in the distance, and by the shore of the village one or two large white manor houses jut skyward through the groves of cypress and wild olive trees. The houses and the trees shimmer in a golden heat haze, gauzy white clouds drift above the sea, dreamy and inconclusive.

AFTERWORD

On July 14, 2021, Carol Christ passed away from cancer in Greece. Her Molivos workshop in 1997 helped my daughter and me grow closer. Sam returned to university and went on to run a literary agency, get married, and have two children while Carol moved to Crete and continued running tours of Minoan shrines.

Carol wrote more books, and so did I. I also co-founded a prize for women and non-binary fiction authors in Canada and the United States. In 2016, I married my common-law partner Patrick Crean, who seemed to intuit the secret wish I described in my 1970s diaries about wanting a marriage proposal from my lover without needing to marry him. At the age of seventy, I finally said yes. I'm in my late seventies now, and Carol isn't here to discuss this new stage, although one evening in Lesbos in 2004, long before she died, she shared her thoughts with me.

She and I were having dinner with my cousin David Cowan and his husband, Jim Bennette, in Vafios, a village near Molivos. I don't bother talking about my spiritual views with most people, and before our meal, I worried that my cousin and his partner might be threatened by Carol's feminist theology. Carol and her philosophy have been attacked by academics in religious studies, including feminist Christians, and I don't want the evening to

deteriorate into hostile exchanges. Instead, David and Jim are
intrigued, and soon the four of us are sharing intimate family
stories over a dinner of fried zucchini flowers and barbounia,
washed down with glasses of homemade retsina.

As we linger over our Nescafé coffees, admiring the view of
the Aegean, the lights in the houses flick off one by one. The
village falls into darkness. The only noise is the sound of a boy
playing with a ball in the cobblestone street. Vafios had once
been a bustling agricultural community with a leather-dying
business. Today, barely more than one hundred inhabitants live
in the village, and more people are leaving every year.

We pay our bill and leave in David's rental, still talking in-
tensely as he drives the car down the steep hillside on the road
leading back to Molivos. One of us asks Carol what she's doing
in the fall, and she tells us she'll be giving a lecture at Harvard
University on Aphrodite.

When she was young, Carol says, she used to take young
women to the ancient temple to Aphrodite in Lesbos near the
bay of Kalloni. They often left offerings to the goddess, naively
hoping Aphrodite would bring them romantic love, and when
Carol's Greek lover left her, Carol blamed the goddess. She became depressed and couldn't write. But now she bemoans the
way she failed to see that Aphrodite represented a broader interpretation of love than Western culture has given the goddess.
The wider interpretation of Aphrodite representing beauty and
enjoyment is in the Greek myths, and Carol said she needed to
get older before she apprehended its meaning. After her depression faded, she became aware of the affectionate caretaking she
had received from her colleagues and friends. It reminded her

that the joy of being together with amiable companions is also part of love. She cites our evening as proof.

Without warning, David puts on the brakes.

A shapeless mass of woolly bodies is blocking the road ahead. In the darkness comes the tinkling of sheep bells. They ring out operatically, sometimes in two pitches. We stop talking to listen. The bells go on for almost ten minutes, and then we drive on.

Acknowledgements

First and foremost, I'd like to thank Margaret Atwood for giving me the idea of writing about a subject that has been literally right under my nose all my life: my Amazonian size. Her flattering description of me posing as classical statues without my clothes may be fanciful, but her story instinct was dead-on.

There's a popular belief that everyone has a book in them. But it's more accurate to say everyone's life is a book. Our personal lives resemble novels because they follow themes that lead us in certain directions, although we aren't always conscious of where we're going or what we're doing. But the story unfolds despite us, and it often yields surprising and dramatic results. My own story is no different.

I'd also like to thank my editor, Jennifer Lambert, for seeing the potential in the conundrum of being a big woman in a culture that has traditionally preferred women not take up much space. And heartfelt thanks to my agent, my daughter, Samantha Haywood, and my husband, Patrick Crean, for their support and guidance during the three years it took me to write this book. And a giant thank-you to others who helped with this book: Amanda Lewis, Anne Collins, and Eva Oakes read different drafts and made helpful editorial comments, as did Isabel Huggan, Anne Mackenzie and Susan Coyne. I also want to thank Chelene Knight, my student Juliann Garisto and my personal assistant Joseph Burdi for reading a draft of the manuscript and offering comments from the perspective of their generation. And thanks, as always, to Alberto Manguel for his ongoing support of my writing and for his interest in my memoir. Every writer needs unwavering champions, and throughout our lives, he has played that role for me.

Big Girls Don't Cry includes previously published sections of pieces I wrote titled "Rest in Power: Carol Christ, the Rebellious Scholar Who Took on the World of Religious Thought" (*Ms. Magazine*, February 15, 2022, https://msmagazine .com/2022/02/15/carol-christ-feminist-scholar-religion) and "Corfu: Visiting Lawrence Durrell's White House (From My Greek Journals)" (in *Writing Away: The PEN Canada Travel Anthology*, ed. Constance Rooke [Toronto: McClelland & Stewart, 1994], 295–306).

The epigraph comes from Michelle Obama's book tour for her memoir *The Light We Carry*, when she was interviewed by Conan O'Brien on December 9, 2022, at the Masonic Temple in San Francisco. The event was made into a podcast with O'Brien on April 4, 2023, titled *Michelle Obama: The Light Podcast*. *The Light Podcast* is produced by Higher Ground and Little Everywhere, a Higher Ground and Audible Original. The quotation on page vii is taken from Michelle Obama's book *The Light We Carry* (New York: Crown, 2022), page 90. The letter quoted on page 221 by Lawrence Durrell is from Lawrence Durrell, *Spirit of Place: Letters and Essays on Travel*, edited by Alan G. Thomas, (E.P. Dutton, 1969), page 43.